James Bond Co
REDUX
Featuring Cold Reading Games

Also by Julian Moore

Palmistry
Palm Readings In Your Own Words

Graphology
The Art Of Handwriting Analysis

Cartomancy
Fortune Telling With Playing Cards

Numerology
Numbers Past And Present With The Lo-Shu Square

Star Signs
A Cool System For Remembering The Dates And Meanings Of The Twelve Signs Of The Zodiac

James Bond Cold Reading
REDUX

Featuring Cold Reading Games

Julian Moore

The Cold Reading Company

DOWNLOAD THE FLASH CARDS,
AUDIO, AND OTHER SUPPORT
DOCUMENTS FROM OUR WEBSITE

WWW.COLDREADING.CO

FREE REGISTRATION

NO PURCHASE REQUIRED

This Book Copyright 2023

Julian Moore /

THE COLD READING COMPANY

JULIAN@COLDREADING.CO

WWW.COLDREADING.CO

Praise For
The James Bond Cold Reading

"I got Julian's book, and it is wonderful! It is a great system for doing a reading and extremely practical. I applaud Julian and highly recommend this!"

Richard Osterlind

"I have tried many times to learn the stock lines of cold reading. I've tried memory techniques, linking, the peg system, and even with all that everything seemed a confusing, repetitive mess. Because of Julian's system, in two days, I have learned to give a cold reading forward, backward, inside-out and in my own words. I feel comfortable enough that anyone at any time could come up to me for a reading and I can just start wailing."

Scott Martisse

"First palmistry, now general Forer-Barnum 101...

This guy really amazes me."

Craig Browning

"It's ingenious, simple, and thought-inspiring, all at the same time! Buy this now and start using it right away!"

R. Lee Davis

"Folks, don't just read The James Bond Cold Reading. Get out there and use it."

Bill Cushman

BEFORE WE START, A FAVOUR

WRITING BOOKS, RECORDING AUDIO, CREATING SUPPORT DOCUMENTS AND HOSTING WEBSITES TAKES A HUGE AMOUNT OF TIME AND DEDICATION.

TRUTH IS, ALTHOUGH I HAVE MY OWN SITE, IT'S AMAZON SALES THAT KEEP ME GOING.

WITHOUT AMAZON RATINGS AND REVIEWS THIS BOOK WILL DISAPPEAR INTO OBSCURITY, AS WILL MY ABILITY TO WRITE MORE BOOKS.

SO PLEASE, IF YOU FIND JAMES BOND COLD READING REDUX USEFUL IN ANY WAY, TAKE A MINUTE TO RATE AND REVIEW THIS BOOK.

RATINGS DRIVE VISIBILITY

REVIEWS DRIVE SALES

'I loved it!' — Alan Reader

THANKS IN ADVANCE FOR ALLOWING ME TO WRITE BOOKS MY WAY, AND FOR HELPING ME KEEP THIS ONE-MAN SHOW ON THE ROAD.

For Alan

Who This Book Is For

If you prefer your readings shaken, not stirred, you've come to the right place; this book double-bill lifts the curtain on cold reading and shows how to deliver entertaining, and impactful, character readings.

- **If you're new to giving readings, this book can get you started.**

- **If you've overdosed on cold reading theory, this book could be the antidote.**

- **And if you're an experienced reader, this book may give you some fresh new ideas.**

Character readings are readings that focus on a person's character rather than their fate–the kind one would expect from a graphologist rather than a soothsayer or psychic. Character readings thus avoid the pitfalls associated with divination and are well tolerated by the public. Skeptics find the allure of a reading harder to resist, when told the future lies in their own hands.

Although people with a passing interest in cold reading may find this book interesting, this is a practical book that requires time and effort to be of any worldly use. Saying that, I believe this book can get you up and running in record time and, with a modicum of effort, you can learn to give entertaining readings in a matter of days.

You Only Live Twice

James Bond Cold Reading REDUX is two books in one

James Bond Cold Reading sheds light on the basics of cold reading and shows how to memorise and utilise the twelve lines of the Classic Reading in a fun and entertaining way. Whether you're an experienced reader looking to spice up your practice or a cold reading newbie, James Bond Cold Reading has something to offer.

Cold Reading Games explains how a little knowledge of Palmistry, Graphology and Numerology can help create conversation and make new friends. Whether or not you're familiar with these skills, Cold Reading Games shows you how to use them to their maximum potential, when combined with the methods found in James Bond Cold Reading.

But wait, there's more!

The new, improved **Bonus Section** now includes:

- **Astrology** - A cool technique to remember and recall the dates of the twelve signs of the zodiac.

- **Cartomancy** - Fortune telling with playing cards, using meanings taken from the Numerology section.

- **Cold Reading As Effect** - A seven page essay on how cold reading can elevate a simple card trick into a powerful demonstration of mind-reading!

There's No Time To Die, so let's get started!

Table Of Contents

Foreword 14

Overview 15

    What Is Cold Reading? 15

    What Is A Character Reading? 16

    What Is James Bond Cold Reading? 17

    Truisms And Traits 17

    Sections And Symbols 19

JAMES BOND COLD READING 21

Original Foreword by Enrique Enriquez 22

Original Introduction By The Author 24

Support Documents 25

The Classic Reading 26

    The Twelve Lines Of The Classic Reading 26

    My Personal Take On The Classic Reading 28

    Mechanics Of A Reading 31

JBCR Method 34

Conceptual Riffing 38

    James Bond Cold Reading Concepts 44

    JBCR Recap 47

Riffing On Bond 50

The James Bond Plot 58

    JBCR - Learning And Application 62

    Speed Learning JBCR 64

Oracular Vernacular 67

    Traditional Oracles With JBCR 67

Non-Traditional Oracles With JBCR 68

    Hot Or Not 69

Shaping A Reading 79

    Introduction (Titles) 79

    Summary (Credits) 80

    Three Act Structure 81

    Lenses Of Time 81

    Inner And Outer Lenses 88

    Structure In A Structure 89

    Lens Within A Lens 90

Lucky Escapes 92

Protaganother 99

The Imaginarium 101

    A Waking Dream 103

JBCR Conclusion 105

COLD READING GAMES 107

Introduction 109

Backstory 115

PALMISTRY 118

P1 Lines Of The Hand 120

    Heart Line 125

    Head Line 131

    Life Line 135

P2 Bringing The Lines Together 139

P3 Finger Meanings 145

P4 The Approach 150

P5 Bringing It All Together 157

P6 Palmistry Reading Practice 167

P7 Palmistry Conclusion 170

GRAPHOLOGY 171

G1 The Letters T & I - Graphology Golf 173

G2 The Letters Y and P - Sociability And Physicality 178

G3 Slants And Baselines 181

G4 Signature 186

G5 The Graphology Approach 191

G6 Bringing It All Together 195

G7 Graphology Reading Example 202

G8 Graphology Reading Practice 205

G9 Graphology Conclusion 208

NUMEROLOGY 209

N1 Number Meanings 210

N2 Life Cycle Basics 211

N3 Life Cycle In Detail 213

N4 Life Cycle Chapters 219

N5 Mobile Number Readings 223

N6 The Approach 224

N7 Bringing It All Together 229

N8 Mobile Number Reading Example 239

N9 Numerology Reading Practice 245

N11 Numerology Conclusion 246

BONUS SECTION 247

Star Signs 248

Cartomancy 265

Cold Reading As Effect 272

Foreword

Welcome to James Bond Cold Reading REDUX featuring Cold Reading Games!

The James Bond Cold Reading (2007) started life as a limited PDF release, and showed how the twelve lines of the Classic Reading can be memorised, and utilised, to give character readings. Popular with magicians and mentalists alike, the original James Bond Cold Reading was an underground hit when released, but did little to explain the mechanics of giving readings outside of a performance.

Cold Reading Games (2014) took an entirely different approach to The James Bond Cold Reading and showed how a little knowledge of Palmistry, Graphology or Numerology could be used to break the ice with strangers. Written for the general public, Cold Reading Games gave laypeople a variety of tools to help initiate conversation during awkward social situations.

James Bond Cold Reading REDUX brings both releases together into one edition for the first time. Cold Reading Games now references James Bond Cold Reading, and James Bond Cold Reading touches on the practical aspects of giving readings found in Cold Reading Games. Each book has been rewritten from the ground up, and both books now cover a great deal more ground than their original versions.

This edition starts with James Bond Cold Reading, but there's nothing to stop you jumping straight into Cold Reading Games. Learning the basics of Palmistry, Graphology or Numerology can be a great start towards giving character readings, and you can always tackle the concepts found in James Bond Cold Reading later, should you wish.

Cold reading takes practice, and baby steps are best when you're starting out. Travel light, take brief trips and refer to the map as infrequently as possible. A little knowledge goes a long way, and the only way to get good is to get going. Best of luck!

Julian Moore

Stackpole, Wales 2023

Overview

Readers, Clients And Oracles

The terms Reader, Client and oracle are used throughout these books:

READER refers to the person giving a reading

If you are performing a reading on someone else you are the Reader

CLIENT refers to the person being given a reading

Anyone having a reading performed on them is the Client

ORACLE refers to the purported method used

Most readers attribute their abilities to an oracle of some kind

Your oracle can be whatever you want it to be: Palmistry, Graphology, 'The Power Of The Mind'–it's up to you. The traditional definition of an oracle is that of a person through whom divination flows such as The Oracle Of Delphi, but in this book the word oracle refers to the method of transmission, either real or implied. You can reference a traditional oracle, such as Palmistry, as the source of your knowledge, or imply that your knowledge of social science is enough to delve into a person's psyche. It's up to you how you frame it.

Throughout this book, the terms Reader and Client are capitalised to help us recognise who's who. Palmistry, Graphology and Numerology are also capitalised, but oracle is not, as oracle could refer to any of these techniques.

What Is Cold Reading?

Cold reading is an umbrella term for a variety of techniques employed by mentalists, fortune tellers and mediums, used to give the impression of a greater than average ability to read the character of another person. The term cold simply means that this is performed cold, i.e. with no previous knowledge of the Client in question.

Although cold reading is not a science as such, it is an attempt to understand the interplay between a Reader and their Client in a scientific way. It could be argued that, although many professional readers have yet to read a book on cold reading, their interpersonal skills have developed over time and have more to do with cold reading than the power of their chosen oracle. Some readers, however, see a knowledge of cold reading as an important part of their practice, and others use it intentionally outside the realm of traditional readings.

For instance:

- A full-time tarot reader may deny the use of cold reading in his own practice, although many of his abilities could be attributed to cold reading.

- A professional palmist could inadvertently develop skills that closely resemble cold reading, and be surprised to discover similar methods in cold reading literature.

- A Graphology expert might knowingly use various cold reading techniques as part of their larger repertoire, including body language and racial profiling.

- A mentalist, billed as a 'Conjurer Of The Mind', may use cold reading techniques in their mind-reading show, to an audience entertained by psychological trickery.

WHAT IS A CHARACTER READING?

A character reading is a reading focused solely on the personality of the Client. During a character reading, the Reader offers statements they feel resonate with the Client regarding the Client's personality. A dialogue ensues, and the hope is that by the end of the reading, apart from being impressed by the Reader's insight, the experience has given the Client some interesting food for thought.

One of the fundamental principles governing the success of a character reading is the Reader's ability to talk in broad terms whilst helping the Client interpret these terms into specific and personal traits. Although character readings are normally delivered via traditional methods, such as

Palmistry, their principles can be worked into everyday conversation to convey a sense of empathy, and connection.

A good example of a vanilla character reading is the type a person could expect from having their handwriting analysed. By studying their Client's handwritten scrawls, a good graphologist hopes not only to tell Clients what they are like, but to shed some light on their subconscious thought processes. Another example of a character reading is the type a Client would experience during a personality-based Palmistry reading. Although character readings offer Clients a chance to pause and reflect on their lives, they do not give advice or make predictions.

At their best, character readings can empower Clients to tread their own, unique path with a sense of optimism, and a good Reader can help Clients answer most of their own questions. At the very least, a Client should take heart that you, the Reader, agree wholeheartedly that they are an outstanding and talented individual.

What Is James Bond Cold Reading?

James Bond Cold Reading (**JBCR**) is a system for learning and delivering a truism based character reading based on the twelve lines of the Classic Reading.

The Classic Reading is not new. Created by psychologist Bertram Forer, these twelve truisms have been reworked and retooled by many readers. However, since the birth of the internet, Forer's work has slowly worked its way into common parlance and the existence of 'Barnum Statements' (another phrase describing truisms named after American showman P. T. Barnum) can be easily found for those with a passing interest in the psychology of readings. James Bond Cold Reading reimagines the Classic Reading using a visual narrative that aids both the recall, and spontaneous delivery, of each line, and reveals just how useful these truisms can be when used as a springboard for the imagination.

Truisms And Traits

Cold reading requires a lot of talking and to talk, you need something to say. The undeniable fact is that most, if not all, readings require the Reader to talk in **truisms**—broad statements that are ripe for interpretation by the Client. 'Some things never change' is a self-evident truism, albeit one not particularly useful one to a Reader. A better one would be 'The apple never falls far from the tree', as it feels personal and a Client can read into it what they like. Platitudes aside, and for the purposes of this book, a truism is an open-ended statement that almost anyone can take personally.

A **trait** is a characteristic of an Client's personality and, although traits can refer to genetic similarities, this book is interested in people's demeanour more than their eye colour. Traits are offered up to Clients during the course of a reading and, unless you are talking to a Bond villain, you will be using attributes such as adaptable, intelligent and modest to boost your Client's morale, rather than ruthless, vindictive, and maniacal.

Here's a list of positive traits that can be helpful during a reading. Browse through them and see which ones you think best describe you.

Adaptable	Faithful	Kind	Respectful
Adventurous	Flexible	Loyal	Responsive
Articulate	Focused	Modest	Romantic
Balanced	Forgiving	Objective	Selfless
Capable	Freethinking	Observant	Self-critical
Caring	Generous	Open	Sensitive
Clear-headed	Genuine	Optimistic	Skilful
Compassionate	Gracious	Passionate	Solid
Conscientious	Hardworking	Peaceful	Spontaneous
Considerate	Honest	Perceptive	Steadfast
Courteous	Honourable	Perfectionist	Strong
Creative	Humble	Persuasive	Sympathetic
Curious	Idealistic	Principled	Tasteful
Deep	Imaginative	Protective	Tolerant
Empathetic	Individualistic	Rational	Trusting
Enthusiastic	Intelligent	Realistic	Understanding
Fair	Intuitive	Reflective	Wise

If you are as humble and selfless as I am, you'll probably agree that most, if not all, of these traits describe you personally in some way or another. People interpret one-word traits much like truisms, and cannot help but see themselves in a positive light when given half a chance.

SECTIONS AND SYMBOLS

To help you identify important information as you flick through these pages, the following section frames and symbols and are used throughout this book:

THE POWER OF IMAGINATION

Sections marked **IMAGINE** require you to spend time visualising.

James Bond Cold Reading relies on the power of imagination, and you will be asked to imagine yourself as James Bond in various scenarios throughout this book. Visualising these scenarios will help you recall the key concepts of JBCR. You will probably need to read through JBCR a few times for it all to sink in, so each IMAGINE exercise is numbered and titled for reference.

Please read this book with an open mind and do what it asks of you. The imagination is a far better sponge than working memory and, by using a fraction of the effort it takes to read a few pages of a novel, you'll be able to recall JBCR in hours rather than days. If you have a passing interest in readings but are not prepared to put these methods to good use, please look elsewhere. This book is a practical guide to giving readings in the real world, not an intellectual exposé for the curious.

Should you find James Bond Cold Reading too abstract at first, dip into Cold Reading Games to get a handle on more traditional oracles such as Palmistry and Graphology. We all learn differently, so hopping between the theory behind JBCR, and the more simplistic approach of CRG, can help you find your feet when starting out.

To remember something for a long time, in the shortest possible time, visualise it.

Get Your Mouth In Gear

It's essential you practice talking out loud, so when you see **Get Your Mouth In Gear** be prepared to speak up! Readings are about talking the talk, not thinking the think, and your readings will only ever be as good as the words that fall from your mouth. **Get Your Mouth In Gear** exercises can help you find your voice so, in the interests of no one but yourself, practice speaking out loud whenever, and wherever, you can.

NUTSHELLS

Nutshells are summaries of earlier sections. These condensed snippets can help you learn more quickly, and are great for second or third read-throughs. They're also a great reference which brings us to...

Photo Opportunities

If you've got a camera on your phone, why not create your own reference material on the fly? The camera symbol is displayed whenever there's a particularly useful chunk of information. Take snaps as you read this book, and refer back to them when needed.

James Bond Cold Reading

You'll find cross-reference info boxes scattered throughout these two books, notifying you of relevant, interesting, and illuminating sections from each book's counterpart.

Cold Reading Games

JAMES BOND COLD READING

Original Foreword by Enrique Enriquez

I am confident that this book will not make you another expert in cold reading. Instead of that, I know this book can effectively turn you into an actual cold reader.

This book deals with a very specific form of cold reading–the delivery of stock phrases, or stock readings. Building on the successful systematization for learning Palmistry that he already shared with the community, Julian Moore is undertaking in this book the not so easy task of giving you the right pointers to do a stock reading that will come out in your own words.

Stock readings are applied fiction. A well-selected plot that you offer to a person, suggesting directly and indirectly that such plot IS the person. After all, each one of us is a crossroad of tales and myths seeking a way to realize themselves. Each one of us is a tale writing itself. "Society" can be defined as a group of people sharing the same tales. Know the society's tale and you will know the people who live in that society.

James Bond movies are not successful because we all want to be like James Bond, but because James Bond is like all of us. Several times along his adventures, we find ourselves in the same mindset as Bond. There is a part of Bond that is human and is his human side that makes his heroic side worthwhile. This is what Julian has capitalized upon–a systematic approach to understanding a basic and well-tested story-line, so you can use it in a way that makes sense and comes out naturally.

Half of what you need to perform powerful cold reading is an understanding of the story-lines that define human nature. The other half is confidence. No one but yourself will give you the later, but Julian can help you with the former. That is why he wrote this book. It is a good thing that you are reading it now!

A little suggestion–don't bother by peeking at your participant's shoes, shopping bags, rings, or fingernails. Forget about picking clues in the way Sherlock Holmes famously did. There is nothing to see in your participant since the effect we call cold reading, when we are using stock lines, isn't something you do to them, but something you help them do by themselves. Don't force it, let it happen! What you are really doing is offering the person a piece of information in a context that suggests that this information is about them.

Therefore, it is up to the person's mind to define the relevance of the information you are delivering. Cold reading is real and powerful magic, because it is magic that happens in the participant's mind. You are giving them permission to re-create themselves through your words. Practice that skill with respect.

There is something intriguing, entertaining, and potentially enlightening in knowing how are we perceived by others. That is why cold reading is so powerful. A performer capable of doing that will always command his audience's attention.

But you know that! Otherwise you would not be reading this book, seduced by the allure that cold reading has over all kinds of mystery performers.

So, are you ready for your mission? Get into the action and remember that if you stand confident under fire, the bullets will not harm you. The party is on. It is time for you to make your move...

Enrique Enriquez

New York, April 2007

ORIGINAL INTRODUCTION BY THE AUTHOR

The original Classic Reading is a list of twelve truisms that can apply to almost anyone. Dating back to the 1940s, these stock lines have often been used in conjunction with traditional oracles such as Palmistry, or used to enhance either magic or mentalism performances.

When researching cold reading, the twelve lines of the Classic Reading are the first thing to catch the attention of the novice. However, on attempting to commit these lines to memory, it becomes apparent they are not only hard to remember, but woefully lacking in context.

My answer to this dilemma is to base the entire Classic Reading on the James Bond character, re-imagining the twelve lines as a character driven story to help remember, and deliver, the lines in a meaningful way. James Bond Cold Reading is both a memory aid, and a visualisation tool, to help the words come more easily. I hope it serves you well.

Julian Moore
Portsmouth UK, May 2007

Support Documents

To help practice and recall the methods used in JBCR, several support documents are available from my website, including James Bond Cold Reading flash cards, a Cold Reading Games cheat sheet, and a selection of audio files to help you learn on the go. These support documents can boost your learning experience and, although not essential for the enjoyment of this book, I urge you to check them out. Print the flash cards onto index cards, or view and listen to both them, and the audio files, on the device of your choice.

Support material is provided free to registered users. No purchase of James Bond Cold Reading REDUX is necessary. Registration is free, takes less than a minute, and grants access to the support documents for all of my books. Should you enjoy what is on offer, I hope you will purchase some of my other books to help support my work.

To access the support documents including flash cards and audio, please register at www.coldreading.co

1

THE CLASSIC READING

Created by the psychologist Bertram Forer in the 1940s, the Classic Reading comprises twelve character traits most people would agree applied to them. In his famous experiment, Forer gave each of his students what they thought was a personalised character reading, with instructions to report back on their accuracy. The students, unaware they'd each been fed identical readings, found them eighty percent accurate, even though Forer had plucked the lines from an inexpensive book of daily horoscopes. Hoodwinked as easily as the general public, Forer's students were mortified.

Since then, stock lines have been developed as business and marketing tools categorised by age, sex and socio-economic status. A male middle-aged divorcee would react differently to the stock lines targeted at a seventy-five-year-old grandma, for example. For the purposes of this book, we're going to stick with Forer's original lines, as they are broad enough to apply to almost anyone. Once you've learnt how to implement the lines of the Classic Reading, you can add more targeted lines as you see fit.

Here are the twelve lines of Forer's Classic Reading, as presented to his students. Put yourself in their shoes for a moment, and take the time to read each line as if it had been tailored to you personally.

THE TWELVE LINES OF THE CLASSIC READING

- At times you are extroverted, affable, sociable, while at other times you are introverted, wary, and reserved.

- You have a strong need for other people to like you and for them to admire you.

- Disciplined and controlled on the outside, you tend to be worrisome and insecure on the inside.

- You have a tendency to be critical of yourself.

- You pride yourself on being an independent thinker and do not accept others opinions without satisfactory proof.

- You have found it unwise to be too frank in revealing yourself to others.

- Your sexual adjustment has presented some problems for you.

- While you have some personality weaknesses, you are generally able to compensate for them.

- At times you have serious doubts as to whether you have made the right decision or done the right thing.

- You prefer a certain amount of change and variety and become dissatisfied when hemmed in by restrictions and limitations.

- Some of your aspirations tend to be pretty unrealistic.

- You have a great deal of unused capacity which you have not turned to your advantage.

I am sure you agree that many of these lines ring true because, although the content of our lives may appear different on the surface, we all tend to think about ourselves in the same way. These are broad concepts and we cannot help but search for meaning, as we seek to connect them with our own internal, and external, experiences.

Take a moment to read through the lines again, and note the traits you feel do not apply to you. I think you'll be hard pressed to find any you strongly disagree with. It will be the same when you attribute these lines to other people.

There now follows a light-hearted take on each line from my own perspective. Before you read through it, go back and take the time to think about how each line of the Classic Reading applies to you personally. Once you've done that, compare your thoughts on each line with mine, and notice how each line resonates with us in different ways.

My Personal Take On The Classic Reading

- **At times you are extroverted, affable, sociable, while at other times you are introverted, wary, and reserved.**

This is me. I write books and spend a lot of time alone making music, but I can only do this for so long before I feel the need to see my friends, socialise, and sometimes party. Those who see me as an extrovert do not see my quieter, reclusive side that much, and even people I work with regularly underestimate how much time I spend alone. I wouldn't say I am particularly reserved, although I can be reserved about certain things.

- **You have a strong need for other people to like you and for them to admire you.**

I like people and I like to be liked, but I have learned you cannot please everyone all the time. Admiration is a tricky one. I do possess a certain amount of professional pride, and the odd bit of praise never went amiss. I've never been that great at taking compliments, so being appreciated will do. Saying that, I would be pretty chuffed to find I have a secret admirer.

- **Disciplined and controlled on the outside, you tend to be worrisome and insecure on the inside.**

Worrisome and insecure on the inside? Completely, but controlled on the outside? Hardly. I don't think I've ever felt disciplined, either on the outside or the inside. I would definitely say that I'm very good at keeping my insecurities to myself, otherwise books would not get written, and neither would any music.

- **You have a tendency to be critical of yourself.**

If I was less critical of myself, I would probably be less worrisome and insecure. I often wish I could turn my internal critic off as it leads to perfectionism, and perfection is most definitely the enemy of good. My internal critic can be exhausting sometimes, and although it can spur me on, it can also get in the way.

- **You pride yourself on being an independent thinker and do not accept others' opinions without satisfactory proof.**

I like to think for myself, or think I do. I'm always fact checking what people say on social media. I sometimes do not think anyone thinks about things in quite the same way as I do. I think I have a unique way of seeing things. I believe experts once I have checked their sources. I know what I do not know, and I am happy to concede to people with greater knowledge.

- **You have found it unwise to be too frank in revealing yourself to others.**

This is probably the one line I feel does not apply to me, as I have always been an open book. Some people keep their cards close to their chest, but mine are usually scattered all over the floor. I don't care too much what other people think about me, so very little I have done can be used against me.

- **Your sexual adjustment has presented some problems for you.**

This line does not ring true either. I don't think I've had any problems in that department. Romantically perhaps, but not sexually. It should be noted that this line benefits from being viewed in a broader context, to include relationships and matters of the heart.

- **While you have some personality weaknesses, you are generally able to compensate for them.**

Some aspects of my personality are definitely weaker than others. I want to believe I have many more strong, unique and wonderful personality traits than weak ones, but that sounds rather pompous and big-headed, both definite signs of weakness. Such a dilemma.

- **At times you have serious doubts as to whether you have made the right decision or done the right thing.**

This becomes frighteningly more applicable the older one gets. In my teens, I was wondering if I should have chosen computer science over music, but in middle age my ability to worry about every decision I have ever made is par for the course. Hindsight is a wonderful thing, and I bash myself around the head with it most days.

- **You prefer a certain amount of change and variety and become dissatisfied when hemmed in by restrictions and limitations.**

This is definitely a line that resonates with me. I routinely fight against routines, even those I have made for myself. I'm all about change and variety, and if I'm not allowed to go somewhere, or do something, I am more than twice as likely to do it. I can be impulsive like that.

- **Some of your aspirations tend to be pretty unrealistic.**

Totally. There is no way sales of this book are going to buy me that yacht I've always wanted. I need to stop kidding myself.

- **You have a great deal of unused capacity which you have not turned to your advantage.**

I feel I've never got my act together to harness my unused capacity. I'm convinced my untapped potential is locked behind a wall of procrastination, disorganisation, and laziness. This thought is not only a constant source of stress, but is one of the ways I regularly berate myself.

So there you have it. Although I may come across as a paranoid bag of nerves, I have tried to be truthful with my answers and it goes to show that, no matter how someone presents themselves in public, you will never truly know what ails them. As a man far wiser than me once said, 'Be kind, for everyone you meet is fighting a hard battle'.

Mechanics Of A Reading

I don't disagree with much that the Classic Reading has to tell me about myself. Its statements are open-ended and its scope broad, so it's hard to disagree with almost anything, give or take a few minor details. If I had no prior experience with cold reading, and you read me these lines today, I am sure they'd work just as well on me as the students in Forer's experiment.

We've already touched on some ways a reading can develop, but let's focus on **two fundamentals** that occur during not only James Bond Cold Reading, but almost any kind of reading:

1. People will attempt to make meaning of your comments by taking them personally

Although I've described how the lines of the Classic Reading resonate with me on a personal level, you'll get far less feedback when you verbalise these lines to other people. It's all but impossible to know how other people connect with what you're saying and, although some lines will hit home more than others, you will mostly never know why. The good news is that your broad comments will be interpreted as specific, just as they were by both me, and you.

Here's how two Classic Reading lines could be interpreted as specific:

- When you said 'your aspirations tend to be pretty unrealistic', you were talking about my dreams of becoming a fashion designer, right?

- When you told me 'you have serious doubts whether you've made the right decision or done the right thing', you were surely talking about me selling the house after my split with Helen.

Human beings cannot help but search for personal meaning to that which is ascribed to them. We reverse engineer the vague into something precise. It is almost impossible for us not to do this. It's all part of the human condition.

2. You can use the feedback you receive from each line to fuel the conversation

Unlike the original Forer experiment, verbalising a line of the Classic Reading to a Client can form the basis of a conversation. If you're lucky, people will tell you what's on their mind, and your dialogue can be tailored accordingly. So, with a little feedback, you can drop inappropriate lines, and expand on others.

Here's an example of an inappropriate line:

> You are attempting a reading for a stranger called Roger at a bar. You tell Roger he's extroverted, affable and sociable, while at other times introverted, wary and reserved.
>
> Roger looks somewhat puzzled before calling out, 'Drinks are on me!' Roger's friends flock to the bar. He seems pretty popular.

This is probably not the time to follow up with the Classic Reading line 'worrisome and insecure on the inside' as there's a good chance Roger is not worrisome or insecure in the slightest. Perhaps a more appropriate follow-up would be 'some of your aspirations tend to be pretty unrealistic'.

This example shows how changing tack, based on environmental and spoken feedback, is key to giving a reading. Pursuing avenues that connect with the Client, sidestepping those that do not, and waltzing brazenly through conversational dead-ends are all fair-game during a reading. A line is only wrong until the next one makes it right and, much like jazz improvisation, cold reading is more about where you're going, than where you've been.

Drawbacks

Although the lines of the Classic Reading have potential as a cold reading framework, they present some problems:

- They lack structure and their concepts are vague, making memorisation difficult.

- The lines are not suitably conversational to be used in a reading.

- Randomly telling strangers what they're like makes little sense.

Solution

James Bond Cold Reading gives you the structure to learn and deliver each line naturally. By weaving a story through the concept of each line, JBCR encourages you to riff on the ideas behind each lines in your own words, rather than parroting each line verbatim and out of context.

2

JBCR Method

James Bond Cold Reading mirrors the Classic Reading, but applies its attributes to James Bond. By reimagining each line as a scene from a Bond film, we can create a script and a plot. By creating these scenes in our mind's eye, the concept of each line is bound to our visual memory so, by recalling a scene, we recall its concept. This inventive and playful way of learning is not only fun, but triggers the same mindset needed when giving readings. The hope is that, with just one sip of an imaginary Martini, you can be ready for action.

Take a moment to compare the JBCR script with the Classic Reading:

James Bond Cold Reading Script A 📷
The 12 Scenes

- You are planning your mission alone, before socialising at the swanky party.
- You are the centre of attention at the party, which you enjoy.
- Although cool and confident, you are nervous about the mission.
- And as a perfectionist, you hope this mission goes according to plan.
- Although you have intelligence about Dr No, you need to find the real truth.
- You cannot be too open, or it would give your identity away.
- Your sexual side has caused its fair share of problems
- Although you have your vices, you are able to compensate in other ways.
- At times, you wonder if being a spy was the correct path for you.
- You prefer change and variety though, so it suits you.
- Some of your plot-lines tend to be pretty unrealistic.
- Even so, you still have some surprises left in you.

The Classic Reading Text
The 12 Lines

- At times you are extroverted, affable, sociable, while at other times you are introverted, wary, and reserved.
- You have a strong need for other people to like you and for them to admire you.
- Disciplined and controlled on the outside, you tend to be worrisome and insecure on the inside.
- You have a tendency to be critical of yourself.
- You pride yourself on being an independent thinker and do not accept others opinions without satisfactory proof.
- You have found it unwise to be too frank in revealing yourself to others.
- Your sexual adjustment has presented some problems for you.
- While you have some personality weaknesses, you are generally able to compensate for them.
- At times you have serious doubts as to whether you have made the right decision or done the right thing.
- You prefer a certain amount of change and variety and become dissatisfied when hemmed in by restrictions and limitations.
- Some of your aspirations tend to be pretty unrealistic.
- You have a great deal of unused capacity which you have not turned to your advantage.

You will notice that JBCR is more concise, and more vague, than the lines of the Classic Reading. This is intentional, giving us less to remember with more focus on the concept behind each line. There is no plot as yet, but we will get to that later.

IMAGINE #1 - Bond vs Classic

Go through each line of JBCR Script A again, putting yourself in James Bond's shoes. Don't try to remember too much for now. Just visualise yourself as Bond, and get a feel for his internal dialogue and his hopes, dreams and concerns. Some lines may appear as scenes, and some may present as voiceovers or monologues. There's no right or wrong way of using your imagination, so relax and see what happens. Spend a good minute visualising each line as vividly as you can.

Once you've spent some time visualising each line of the JBCR Script, browse each line alongside its Classic Reading equivalent below, and familiarise yourself with how each line mirrors its partner.

JAMES BOND COLD READING SCRIPT B
alongside the Classic Reading for reference

1. You are planning your mission alone, before socialising at the swanky party. *At times you are extroverted, affable, sociable, while at other times you are introverted, wary, and reserved.*

2. You are the centre of attention at the party, which you enjoy. *You have a strong need for other people to like you and for them to admire you.*

3. Although cool and confident, you are nervous about the mission. *Disciplined and controlled on the outside, you tend to be worrisome and insecure on the inside.*

4. And as a perfectionist, you hope this mission goes to plan. *You have a tendency to be critical of yourself.*

5. Although you have intelligence about Dr No, you need to find the real truth. *You pride yourself on being an independent thinker and do not accept others' opinions without satisfactory proof.*

6. You cannot be too open or it would give your identity away. *You have found it unwise to be too frank in revealing yourself to others.*

7. Your sexual side has caused its fair share of problems. *Your sexual adjustment has presented some problems for you.*

8. Although you have your vices, you are able to compensate in other ways. *While you have some personality weaknesses, you are generally able to compensate for them.*

9. At times, you wonder if being a spy was the correct path for you. *At times you have serious doubts as to whether you have made the right decision or done the right thing.*

10. **You prefer change and variety though, so it suits you.** *You prefer a certain amount of change and variety and become dissatisfied when hemmed in by restrictions and limitations.*

11. **Some of your plot-lines tend to be pretty unrealistic.** *Some of your aspirations tend to be pretty unrealistic.*

12. **Even so, you still have some surprises left in you.** *You have a great deal of unused capacity which you have not turned to your advantage.*

> ### IMAGINE #2 - JBCR Script B
>
> Re-read JBCR Script B line by line, visualising yourself as Bond in each scene. Consider how the concepts of the JBCR Script and the Classic Reading overlap. If it helps, close your eyes after reading each line. As before, see how vivid you can make each visualisation and bear in mind that, the more you repeat the process, the longer your memories will last.

Feel free to return to this chapter as many times as you like, repeating the exercises **IMAGINE #1** and **IMAGINE #2** until you have a head full of James Bond. Reading the lines backwards, in sets of four, or in a completely random order can help keep things fresh with subsequent passes. At first, it matters very little what you can recall, and your thoughts may all blur into one. You are sewing the seeds of an imagined world you can return to when needed, and subsequent trips will both reinforce, and expand, your memories as you contemplate each concept. Spaced repetition is key, so keep coming back for more.

> **TOP TIP: Don't try to remember everything. Read the lines, visualise yourself in each scene, then forget about them. Building memories is very different to learning lines by rote. Don't be too hard on yourself.**

3

Conceptual Riffing

In musical terms, a riff is one of several pet phrases a guitarist can incorporate into a solo. Riffing is both the development of, and improvisation between, these musical moments to create the illusion of an almost seamless performance. Riffs are both functional and inspirational, and allow the performer to experiment freely, safe in the knowledge that there's always another riff to fall back on. Some guitarists have hundreds of riffs to draw upon, some original, some lifted wholesale from other players. With a catalogue of riffs at their disposal, a talented guitarist can launch into a solo at will.

Conceptual Riffing is about remembering the key concept behind each James Bond Cold Reading scene (riff) and improvising around them in your own words (riffing). Describing these concepts to a Client in your own words takes practice, but will always sound more natural than parroting traits from a list. You cannot predict a Client's reaction to what falls from your mouth, but you can turn to another riff should the current riff fall flat, or run its natural course. After a time, jumping from one riff to the next can feel fluid. The framework of JBCR allows you to embrace the unpredictable, and to see where it takes you.

To show how this works in practice, let's take the first line of JBCR as an example: *'You are planning your mission alone, before socialising at the swanky party.'*

If you've been practicing the exercises in this book, you'll have visualised this first scene already. When you close your eyes and recall it now, how does it appear? When I visualise this scene, I see myself as Bond getting suited and booted in my lavish hotel room, adjusting my cuff-links and inspecting my gadgets while perusing photos and documents of the people important to the mission. Breaking this down further I could say that, as Bond, I enjoyed this time alone, but I'm looking forward to the party. I enjoy being alone but I also enjoy socialising.

How I felt as Bond in my imagination is pretty close in meaning to this first Classic Reading line. Wary of the villains I may encounter, introverted with my multitude of state secrets, and reserved like an English gentleman. At the party I will be sociable, even affable, and although extroversion is not necessarily in my nature, I know when to turn it on should I need it. Surely the very definition of a secret agent is an introverted extrovert!

By wrapping this truism in a scene, we need only imagine ourselves as Bond in our imaginary hotel room to recall the entire concept. I'd wager you will never forget this made-up moment as, when we imagine things with sufficient effort, it is almost impossible to forget them.

So we have the riff, but what can we do with it, and how do we deliver it? Forget about James Bond for a moment and concentrate on you, the person reading this book. How truthful would you say this statement is about you?

> *'I'd imagine you can be sociable, but like downtime to do your own thing. I'm not saying you're an extrovert, but I'm sure you've let your hair down occasionally. Your own personal projects require that you spend time alone. You can be wary of people impeding your plans, but need to find a balance between going out or staying in. I think you'd prefer it if you could be more consistent between your me-time and fun-time. You've learned not to trust everybody, but you can be fun to be around if you want to.'*

The above statement was my **Conceptual Riff** on the concepts behind this first scene of JBCR. I imagined myself as Bond in the hotel room, which brought with it the tangle of ideas, images and truisms I had previously visualised. I used these ideas to start a dialogue and did my best to explain it in my own words, as various elements of the scene came back to me. Rather than offering James Bond my thoughts, I relayed them to you, the reader of this book, as if they applied to you.

When you come to use JBCR in the real world, you will verbalise your thoughts to your Client with no mention of James Bond and his adventures, just as I did for you.

There is certainly nothing special about my short conceptual riff example, but it does show how JBCR can help you learn, recall, and deliver just one line of the Classic Reading in a conversational manner. By giving just a small amount of thought to each scene of JBCR, you will recall truisms at will and start riffing in seconds. Over time, these concepts will become reinforced, your visualisations will get stronger and you will have a greater pool of ideas to draw from. You'll need nothing like as many hours of practice as a guitarist, and a time will come when riffing on a handful of James Bond concepts feels natural.

> **TOP TIP: Your internal struggle to find things to say may be nerve-wracking when starting out, but to a Client it looks like you're simply doing the work of a Reader. Clients have no idea what to expect during a reading, and will interpret your longer pauses as thoughtful interludes, rather than panic-stricken silences.**

Here's another example of riffing on the first line of JBCR, delivered by Dave to a chatty and open Client called Joan.

Dave: *'I imagine you can be sociable, but like downtime to do your own thing. I'm not saying you're an extrovert, but I'm sure you've let your hair down occasionally. Your own personal projects require that you spend time alone.'*

Joan: <shaking head> *'I hardly get any time alone'*

Dave: *'But you can be wary of people getting in the way of your plans, can't you?'*

Joan: *'I guess so, I have to deal with a lot of people. I manage a dance troupe at the weekends.'*

Dave: *'Ah I see. Perhaps you just need to find a better balance*

> between going out or staying in. I think you'd prefer it if you could be more consistent between your me time, and fun time.'

Joan: *'That's true. My girls are always saying that.'*

Dave: *'Perhaps what I'm seeing here is someone who could manage their time better. It could be that you need to spend more time alone, so you can properly organise the stuff you've got on your plate.'*

Joan: *'Millie always says I should get a secretary.'*

Dave: *'Couldn't you get her to do it?'*

Joan: <laughs> *'She's only six, but she has offered already.'*

Dave: *'Quite a responsibility. I can imagine you've learned not to trust everybody. You seem to do most of this stuff yourself.'*

Joan: *'That's true. I've learned to stand on my own two feet.'*

Dave: *'I can see that, but you can be fun to be around. I think you know how to have fun.'*

Joan: *'You bet! The dancers are a crazy bunch, but we have a great time.'*

Even though this is a fictionalised conversation, it shows the mileage you can get from riffing on just one line of JBCR. People are not always this chatty and some may say very little. However, unlike the somewhat confrontational one-liners of the Classic Reading, it's hard to disagree with a stream of consciousness such as this.

If you're still not convinced of the power of James Bond Cold Reading, I'd like you to consider that Tarot cards act much like scenes. The mere thought of a Tarot card triggers a wave of ideas, memories and concepts in the mind of a professional Tarot reader, and a scene from JBCR can have the same effect. The exercises in this book can turn you into a walking, talking, truism machine. Set aside a few minutes a day to visualise and verbalise each scene, and you'll be on your way in no time.

> **TOP TIP:** For any line or concept, the trick is to keep explaining until you have run out of words. See how long you can talk for. Use each line or concept as the basis for a stream of consciousness.

Get Your Mouth In Gear Basics   GYMIG

You need to put yourself on the spot before someone else does, so it's essential you practice conceptual riffing out loud. You may find it surprising how much confidence you can gain from telling inanimate objects about themselves. Family pets and pot plants may not answer back, but they're an excellent substitute for real people when starting out. You can even flick through a magazine and give imaginary readings to the celebrities, models and stars on its pages. Do everything you can to simulate a real-world reading so, when it comes to it, you aren't frozen in the spotlight.

To help you get started, imagine there's a Client standing before you with a burning need to be told what they're like. Read any scene of James Bond Cold Reading to yourself, and attempt to explain to this imaginary person, out loud and in your own words, how the ideas behind this scene could apply to them. Give your imaginary Client space to react by talking slowly and leaving gaps, sometimes big ones, between riffs.

Pauses give you time to think, whilst also allowing the Client to fill the gap themselves. Silence is golden, but also awkward, and can spur Clients on to talk more frequently. If you can, imagine how each of your imaginary Clients react to your riffs during these gaps.

Dicey Business

You can use a die to mimic a Client's response to your riffs. Use low numbers to indicate negative reactions, and higher numbers more positive reactions. After you've exhausted a riff simply roll the die, and change tack depending on your imaginary Client's reaction and feedback.

Roll	Reaction
1	Says nothing
2	Negative reaction
3	Ambivalent reaction on the negative side
4	Ambivalent reaction on the positive side
5	Positive reaction
6	Overwhelmingly positive reaction

If you don't have a die, use playing cards or numbered slips of paper. Generating random responses can give you a great deal of confidence, and I urge you to practice like this from the outset. There'll be more about how to react to Client feedback later in this book, but you may as well start thinking about it now.

On The Record

A great way to simulate being put on the spot is to record your riffs on your phone and, if you're feeling really brave, to video yourself. There's something uniquely terrifying about committing a performance to audio or video, and this simple act can simulate much of the anxiety felt before, and during, a real-world reading. You can also return to your recordings to assess your progress. Hearing or seeing yourself attempt a reading can be deeply unnerving at first, but can go a long way to making you comfortable with the whole procedure. It can also help iron out your strengths and weaknesses. For instance, you may notice yourself talking too fast, or realise there are too few gaps in your delivery. You may even decide to alter the pitch of your voice. These things may only come to light after hearing yourself back, so do not overlook this powerful practice technique.

> **TOP TIP:** If you're not Getting Your Mouth In Gear behind closed doors, you'll struggle to say anything to anyone in the real world. Fake it till you make it.

James Bond Cold Reading Concepts

contrasted with those found in the Classic Reading

Let's take another look at James Bond Cold Reading, and how the James Bond story can remind us of the concepts found in the Classic Reading.

1. You are planning your mission alone, before socialising at the swanky party. *James Bond lives a double-life, spending a lot of time alone quietly planning his next move, before going out there and mingling with the in-crowd. Most people need solitude and socialising in regular doses.*

2. You are the centre of attention at the party, which you enjoy. *James Bond needs attention and admiration, even though it can be his undoing. Most people need to feel liked and, although they may not admit it, quite enjoy a little admiration.*

3. Although cool and confident, you are nervous about the mission. *James Bond is the king of bravado. His steely exterior belies the complex and emotional nature he must keep to himself in order to succeed. Nearly everybody projects a public face while keeping their insecurities in check. Even the toughest looking people can be a bag of nerves.*

4. And as a perfectionist, you hope this mission goes to plan. *James Bond is his own harshest critic. He demands a lot from himself, as we do from ourselves. Being tough on ourselves can get us where we want to be, but it can also be our undoing.*

5. Although you have intelligence about Dr No, you need to find the real truth. *The Bond films are all about what James discovers during the unfolding story. Starting with little information, he finds his own way and the real truth. His independence is the key to finding the facts. Many of us like to think of ourselves as independent, and most of us like to figure things out for ourselves.*

6. You cannot be too open or it would give your identity away. *If James Bond was too open about who he was, he would not get very far, but when the time is right, he knows when to open up. This is from experience, and many of us have regretted revealing too much about ourselves to others.*

7. Your sexual side has caused its fair share of problems. *James Bond's sexual nature has certainly got him into some difficult situations. Sexuality and romance can be confusing and problematic through adolescence and beyond, so this sweeping statement is definitely the most open-ended on the list! Note that the Classic Reading states 'sexual adjustment', but I think it helps to think of this as 'sexual and romantic adjustment'.*

8. Although you have your vices, you are able to compensate in other ways. *James Bond certainly has his vices but his other traits more than make up them. We are all the sum of our parts and, hopefully at least, our strengths make up for our weaknesses.*

9. At times you wonder if being a spy was the correct path for you. *James Bond often doubts his chosen career path and is often confronted with conflicting choices. We often question if we have made the right choices in our careers, romances, and all things spiritual. It is not unusual for people to spend much of their lives wondering whether they have done the right thing.*

10. You prefer change and variety though so it suits you. *Change and variety are the stuff of counter-terrorism and espionage. Although some of us do not embrace change as much as others, nobody enjoys feeling stuck and even people who love their work and life need to mix it up once in a while.*

11. Some of your plot-lines tend to be pretty unrealistic. *Bond films and books have some of the most unrealistic and fantastical plot-lines going. People who want to be like James Bond have ideas above their station, and we all dream a little too big sometimes.*

12. Even so, you still have some surprises left in you. *James Bond ALWAYS has a surprise left in store, even when he is in the tightest corner. Most people have hidden abilities which they have not yet drawn upon. We all like to think we have got a little in reserve, no matter how old we are.*

Using James Bond to drive the narrative gets us away from the rigidity of the Classic Reading, and helps breathe some humanity into each concept. Translating each scene to the Client in your own words may feel like hard work, but it is far better (and more practical) than spitting out two-dimensional Classic Reading lines. The more time and effort you put into visualising each scene, the more you will have to draw upon when you come to give a reading.

Read this chapter a few times, repeating the visualisations as you contemplate each line. Don't expect to remember everything the first time around. Just repeat the visualisations and give some thought to each scene.

> ## IMAGINE #3 - James Bond Cold Reading Concepts
>
> Go back and visualise each of these lines again while considering how James Bond mirrors the hopes, dreams and fears of us all. Consider how each scene relates to you personally, and imagine relaying these thoughts and ideas to a Client. Be thoughtful, reflective and curious, and give yourself as much time with each scene as you deem necessary. See how much you can expand on each concept and, if you are worried you may forget any insights you may experience, write them down.

Here are some additional techniques to help you remember what you've learned so far:

- **Re-read each chapter out loud, and get used to the sound of your own voice.**

- **Try changing your internal perspective during each read-through. A fly on the wall, a security camera, and even one of Bond's accomplices would see each scene differently. Your mind's eye is both versatile and mobile, so make use of it.**

- **Experiment with changing the setting to reflect different Bond eras, from Sean Connery to the present day.**

> **TOP TIP:** A collection of your own riffs can be a very useful tool. Over time, you will find the words come naturally, but compiling a collection of personal riffs is a great way to start.

JBCR Recap

Revision One
Get Your Facts Straight 📝

Here's the JBCR script with its Classic Reading counterparts. Which line pairs with which?

Lines 1 - 4

1. You are planning your mission alone, before socialising at the swanky party.

2. You are the centre of attention at the party, which you enjoy.

3. Although cool and confident, you are nervous about the mission.

4. And as a perfectionist, you hope this mission goes to plan.

A. Disciplined and controlled on the outside, you tend to be worrisome and insecure on the inside.

B. At times you are extroverted, affable, sociable, while at other times you are introverted, wary, and reserved.

C. You have a tendency to be critical of yourself.

D. You have a strong need for other people to like you and for them to admire you.

Answers: 1B 2D 3A 4C

Lines 5 - 8

1. Although you have intelligence about Dr No, you need to find the real truth.

2. You cannot be too open or it would give your identity away.

3. Your sexual side has caused its fair share of problems.

4. Although you have your vices, you are able to compensate in other ways.

A. While you have some personality weaknesses, you are generally able to compensate for them.

B. Your sexual adjustment has presented some problems for you.

C. You pride yourself on being an independent thinker and do not accept others opinions without satisfactory proof.

D. You have found it unwise to be too frank in revealing yourself to others.

Answers: 1C 2D 3B 4A

Lines 9 - 12

1. At times you wonder if being a spy was the correct path for you.

2. You prefer change and variety though so it suits you.

3. Some of your plot-lines tend to be pretty unrealistic.

4. Even so, you still have some surprises left in you.

A. You prefer a certain amount of change and variety and become dissatisfied when hemmed in by restrictions and limitations.

B. Some of your aspirations tend to be pretty unrealistic.

C. You have a great deal of unused capacity which you have not turned to your advantage.

D. At times, you have serious doubts as to whether you have made the right decision or done the right thing.

Answers: 1D 2A 3B 4C

Revision Two
Get Your Mouth In Gear

Visualise the following scenes and attempt to come up with at least one conceptual riff for each. You need to speak out loud and in your own words for this, so you may find it difficult at first. Turn to the next chapter for inspiration should you need it and, if you're finding it easy, see how long you can talk for!

1. You are planning your mission alone, before socialising at the swanky party.

2. You are the centre of attention at the party, which you enjoy.

3. Although cool and confident, you are nervous about the mission.

4. And as a perfectionist, you hope this mission goes to plan.

5. Although you have intelligence about Dr No, you need to find the real truth.

6. You cannot be too open or it would give your identity away.

7. Your sexual side has caused its fair share of problems.

8. Although you have your vices, you are able to compensate in other ways.

9. At times, you wonder if being a spy was the correct path for you.

10. You prefer change and variety though, so it suits you.

11. Some of your plot-lines tend to be pretty unrealistic.

12. Even so, you still have some surprises left in you.

4

Riffing On Bond

Although it's essential you practice Conceptual Riffing in your own words, here are some of my own riffs to get you going. Please note, it is important you riff on concepts rather than recalling specific lines. James Bond Cold Reading is an extemporisation tool, and learning any of these riffs as written would go against the entire principle of this book. However, you can use this section as a reference for when you can't quite establish what to say, or need help expanding the ideas behind a particular scene.

James Bond Cold Reading Riffs

1. You are planning your mission alone, before socialising at the swanky party. *James Bond always lives this double-life where he spends a lot of time alone quietly planning his next move, before getting out there and mingling with the in-crowd. Most people need solitude and socialising in regular doses.*

You could say:

- Sometimes you like to scheme alone and not let people into your private world, but after a while this can become too much and you like to let your hair down and mingle.
- You can be sociable, but like private time to do your own thing.
- You have an independent streak which others can see in you, but you do not let it impede your family and friends.
- Although people think you have a tendency to jump into things, secretly you are a little more reserved than that and give things more thought than people would give you credit for.
- There is always a need for you to charge your batteries and have some 'me' time, although you can have fun when you want to.

- You know when to stop, when it's good for you.
- Some people do not think you have a plan, but you do, of sorts, even though it may not fit in with their own plans!

2. You are the centre of attention at the party, which you enjoy. *James Bond loves the attention and admiration, even though it can be his undoing sometimes. Most people are like this, even the quietest people like attention.*

You could say:

- Sometimes you feel under-appreciated and feel that people do not understand how hard you try.
- Even though you can be shy, you do like to be the centre of attention.
- Some people think you are an attention seeker but you just want to be noticed.
- You are proud of your achievements but unfortunately this can rub some people up the wrong way.
- You are a people person in as much as you like to be needed, and some respect would not go amiss either!
- You enjoy other people's company when it's right for you.
- Although you are humble, you do feel that people to look up to you sometimes.

3. Although cool and confident, you are nervous about the mission. *James Bond is the king of bravado. His steely exterior belies the complex and emotional nature he must keep to himself in order to succeed. He is only human, after all.*

You could say:

- To many people, you do things effortlessly, although you have your own worries.
- Sometimes you find it hard to let your guard down and let people see your own insecurities.
- You have learnt that in order to succeed you must often keep yourself to yourself.
- Showing your genuine emotions has sometimes been a problem for you as you try to be there for everyone else.

- You have an inner determination that can keep you going no matter how tough things appear.
- Friends see you as a shoulder to cry on although sometimes you'd like to borrow theirs!
- You have had to keep your feelings to yourself sometimes so as not to upset other people.

4. And as a perfectionist, you hope this mission goes according to plan. *James Bond is his own harshest critic. He demands a lot from himself. Just like we all do of ourselves, sometimes with tough consequences.*

You could say:

- You can often be your worst critic, and can often hear praise as putdown.
- You like things to be just so, and this has caused some friction in your life.
- You always hope for the best but secretly always try to be better.
- You sometimes worry about where you are going and blame yourself too much for the way your life has gone.
- Even when you achieve great things, you rarely give yourself the credit you deserve.
- You should not expect everyone to live up to the demands you make from yourself.
- You are a perfectionist, even if to some people it does not come across like that.

5. Although you have intelligence about Dr No, you need to find the real truth. *The James Bond films are all about what James discovers during the unfolding story. Starting with little information, he finds his own way and the real truth behind the plot-line. His independence is the key to finding the facts.*

You could say:

- Although you can be a good listener, you like to make your own mind up about things.
- Knowing what is really going on is important to you, but sometimes this can land you in trouble.

- You have always had a longing and are always searching for your own truth.
- You are not easily swayed and can make your own decisions.
- You can be quite stubborn and often take a lot of convincing.
- Sometimes your sense of pride can get in the way of thinking clearly.
- You like to mull over the finer details before coming to conclusions, however this does not mean you are slow to act when you think you are right.

6. You cannot be too open or it would give your identity away. *If James Bond was too open about who he was, he would not get very far. However, when the time is right, he knows when to open up.*

You could say:

- Although you are quite an open person, you have learnt to be cautious.
- You have learnt through experience that you cannot trust everybody and it is not always wise to wear your heart on your sleeve.
- Sometimes you have 'let people in' too soon and have later regretted it.
- Although you are a naturally strong-willed person, you can often wonder who you really are.
- There is a lot going on underneath the surface with you, and only people that you have really got to know will ever see that side of you.
- Some people think they know you but they barely scratch the surface.
- Like most people, you have had your fair share of knock, so you choose your friends carefully before divulging your innermost thoughts and fears.

7. Your sexual side has caused its fair share of problems. *I think it's true to say that James Bond's sexual nature has got him into some difficult situations.*

You could say:

- Sometimes you have found members of the opposite sex to be a genuine mystery.

- Matters of the heart have challenged and perplexed you in the past, however I feel you are coming to a new level of understanding about life, love and the opposite sex.
- I see a time when you did not quite feel comfortable with your sexuality and who you are, but as you have grown, you have learnt to love yourself and others in your own way.
- Some of the confusion of your teenage years with boyfriends/girlfriends is still with you and sometimes you still feel you are not sure what you are doing.
- Although you are quite a passionate person, sometimes you can find it difficult to express it emotionally.
- Your love life has often confused you and created conflicting emotions.
- Your need to be wanted and loved has sometimes attracted the wrong type of person into your life.

8. Although you have your vices, you are able to compensate in other ways. *James Bond has enough vices to clamp the whole of Western Europe. But we love him for it, and he makes up for it in other ways. Bond is only human, after all.*

You could say:

- You can be rather hasty with some things that you find annoying, however you can spend hours doing things you really love.
- You know you are not perfect but feel that you make up for this in other ways that some people do not appreciate.
- You know what you like and can be compulsive sometimes, but this does not mean you do not have restraint, you are just picky about when to use it.
- You do a lot of good in your life, although you worry about even the smallest imperfections.
- Giving yourself a hard time about things can waste a lot of time, even though you know that you more than make up for your shortcomings.
- There are things you wish you could be better and more talented at and this sometimes prevents you from seeing the good you do in other areas.

- Nobody's perfect and you would be the first to agree about that even though sometimes you can find it hard to admit your own imperfections.

9. At times you wonder if being a spy was the correct path for you. *James Bond often has doubts about his chosen career path and is often confronted with conflicting choices. This is the humanity which makes him so endearing as a character.*

You could say:

- You have a tendency to reflect on the past a little too much sometimes.
- Making choices can be a cause of concern for you as you know that in the past you have not always made the best of choices.
- You should not worry too much about the paths you have taken in your life. They all happen for a reason and are leading you to quite a good place.
- If you were to worry less about so of the more dubious decisions you have made up to know, you could enjoy the present a lot more.
- The grass is always greener on the other side and sometimes you wonder what it may be like to be in someone else's shoes.
- You can be worrisome, and the past can trouble you sometimes.
- You cannot change the past, so you should stop worrying about it and move into the future happy and confident that all things have led to the present moment.

10. You prefer change and variety though, so it suits you. *James Bond obviously prefers change and variety and hates being told what to do, even on an important mission! He has defied his orders many times but been proven right just as many.*

You could say:

- You like your home comforts, but a little excitement now and again would not go amiss.
- You have always been unconventional, and sometimes not in ways that anyone would notice readily.

- Freedom is important to you and you do not always feel comfortable being told what to do.
- Although you know when to hold your cool, you have sometimes thought of yourself as a quiet rebel.
- Being able to do what you want when you want is important to you, although life sometimes just does not comply.
- You may have noticed that when you become miserable or disheartened, it is often because you feel trapped and this may go back to feelings you had when you were younger.
- Sometimes you have had to oppose what other people may see as right or wrong, simply to ensure that people do not get hurt.

11. Some of your plot-lines tend to be pretty unrealistic. *Of course, the Bond films and books have some of the most unrealistic and fantastical plot-lines going. People who want to be like James Bond are also having ideas above their station!*

You could say:

- You have a tendency to fantasise somewhat about what may happen in your life.
- You are not a typical dreamer, although you have done your fair share of wishful thinking.
- Sometimes the realities of everyday life can bore you and you can find yourself hoping for some magic wand to change the way things are.
- You can be quite stubborn and find it difficult to admit when you have had ideas above your station.
- You have learnt the hard way that sometimes trying to be what you are not can be painful, however you keep on trying and that is a good thing.
- When you are trying so hard to be good at things you think you should be good at, you can forget how good you are at things you already know.
- Even though you will achieve a lot of your dreams and goals, you're going to have to learn to prioritise those that are most important to you.

12. Even so, you still have some surprises left in you. *James Bond ALWAYS has a surprise left in store, even when he is in the tightest corner. Most people have hidden abilities which they have not drawn upon in their lives.*

You could say:

- You are yet to fully capitalise on all of your talents, some which have laid dormant for many years.
- I feel that you have many abilities that are hiding until the time is right.
- Although you are quite a giving person, you would probably have more to give if you could unlock some of your hidden potential.
- Sometimes you are so busy thinking about the here and now that you forget just how resourceful you can be.
- You do not need to look outward for anything that you need as you have everything right there inside you, even though some of it seems locked away or hard to get at.
- It can be frustrating when you have so many ideas and find it hard to focus on any of them.
- You can be a source of frustration to your friends who see your potential, although most of the time you are blissfully unaware of it.

5

THE JAMES BOND PLOT

The final piece of the puzzle is to weave an overarching plot through James Bond Cold Reading. Linking the end of each scene to the start of the next acts not just as a memory aid, but also enables us to jump seamlessly from one scene to the next. This is far easier than memorising a series of disconnected lines.

To cement the plot sequence in your mind, you need to visualise strong transitions. For instance, 'Bond gets ready alone (before walking down the sweeping staircase) to enjoy the party' is far more memorable than having Bond simply walking through a door, or getting in a lift, to the party. If you struggle to remember a particular line, make a note to create a more vivid transition from the previous line.

Here's the plot I use. Create your own should you wish. It doesn't matter what you come up with as long as you can remember it. No one else will know how you string your script lines together.

Lines 1 - 4

1. You are planning your mission alone, before socialising at the swanky party.

You are in your hotel room going through your mission documents which are contained in your hi-tech briefcase, planning your mission alone before locking up the secrets safely and hiding the briefcase under the bed. You then put your jacket on and take a quick look in the mirror before taking the stairs down to the drinks reception.

The James Bond Plot | 59

2. You are centre of attention at the party, which you enjoy.

Your acquaintances and admirers quickly surround you, and you can soon shake off the thoughts of your mission a little as you relax into the mood of the evening. As always, you are comfortable in this environment.

3. Although cool and confident, you are nervous about the mission.

You cannot totally shake off the thoughts of the mission. However, the memories of the documents and what you have to achieve are never far from your mind. Some people eye you suspiciously from across the room, making you feel a little uneasy.

4. And as a perfectionist, you hope this mission goes to plan.

Like all your missions, there is no margin for error. Only by being meticulous can you ensure everything goes according to plan. You brush off a small piece of fluff from your collar and adjust your tie.(link...)

> *1 - 4 Synopsis: You get ready alone, and enjoy the party, while trying to keep your cool, as you worry about the success of the mission.*

Lines 5 - 8

5. Although you have intelligence about Dr No, you need to find the real truth.

Getting your wallet out of your jacket pocket, you open it and take a quick look at a photograph of Dr No to refresh your memory. You have been told he runs this hotel from a secret basement, but you need to determine this for yourself.

6. You cannot be too open or it would give your identity away.

A young lady strolls over to you from across the room. You quickly hide the photo and put the wallet back in your pocket. One slip of your true identity would be a mistake at this point.

7. Your sexual side has caused its fair share of problems.

She is quite attractive, and you wonder if she is some kind of bait. You have had problems with women in the past. She requests a light for her cigarette.

8. Although you have your vices, you are able to compensate in other ways.

You light her cigarette, but instead of taking one from her, you pull out a nicotine chewing gum and start chewing on it. You have been trying to kick the habit for years but it has always been difficult to avoid it.

5 - 8 Synopsis: You need to find the truth, while not giving your identity away, so flirting, and other vices must be overcome.

Lines 9 - 12

9. At times you wonder if being a spy was the correct path for you.

The lady walks off and you pause to reflect on the past, the adventures, the excitement. Perhaps you should have settled down with a nice lady like that, you wonder.

10. You prefer change and variety though so it suits you.

No sooner have you thought that an absolute stunning leggy blonde who must be without a doubt your next 'Bond Girl' walks into the room to the turning of heads.

11. Some of your plot-lines tend to be pretty unrealistic.

The 'Bond Girl' walks over to you and introduces you to her entourage of ninja-dwarves who are breeding a super-race of man-eating guinea pigs in a desperate bid to conquer the universe.

12. Even so, you still have some surprises left in you.

However, you reach into your back pocket and bring out some 'Ninja-Be-Gone' spray and within a few seconds, you have banished the entire troupe.

9 - 12 Synopsis: You wonder if you've chosen the right path but variety suits you and, although you can be idealistic, you can still surprise yourself sometimes.

The plot slips into nonsense near the end, to illustrate the need for memorable visualisations. If your mental images for each plot line are too similar they'll merge into one, so you'll need to spice things up a little should certain lines fail to stick. The first mental image that comes to mind is often the best and most memorable, and it doesn't matter if it's nonsensical. Choose images that give the best bang for the buck.

IN A NUTSHELL
Here's an abbreviated version of The James Bond Plot.

You get ready alone, before enjoying the party whilst trying to keep your cool as you worry about the success of the mission. You need to find the truth while not giving your identity away, so flirting and other vices must be overcome to succeed. You wonder if you have chosen the right path but variety suits you and, although you can be idealistic, you can still surprise yourself sometimes.

Now do the whole thing in reverse. Read through the breakdown of each line below and visualise each scene you have attached to each of them, noting which scenes appear the most vivid, and which need some work.

You get ready alone

and enjoy the party

while trying to keep your cool

as you worry about the success of the mission.

You need to find the truth

while not giving your identity away

so flirting

and other vices must be overcome to succeed.

You wonder if you have chosen the right path

but variety suits you and,

although you can be idealistic

you can still surprise yourself sometimes.

JBCR - Learning And Application

Let's remind ourselves how James Bond Cold Reading can help us learn, recall and use the concepts behind the twelve lines of the Classic Reading to give a character reading.

Learning JBCR

Learning JBCR is quicker, easier and more fun than committing the twelve lines of the Classic Reading to memory, and provides a framework for memorising each line's concept, rather than the lines themselves. By visualising each element of JBCR for sufficient time, we create memories embedded with truisms that can be recalled at a later date.

There are twelve Classic Reading lines

For instance, 'At times you are extroverted, affable, sociable, while at other times you are introverted, wary, and reserved'

Each line is condensed into a script line from an imaginary Bond scene

For instance, 'You are planning your mission alone, before socialising at the swanky party'.

We visualise ourselves as Bond in each scene whilst adding unique and memorable details

For instance, 'You are in your hotel room going through your mission documents, which are contained in your hi-tech briefcase, planning your mission alone before locking up the secrets safely before hiding the briefcase under the bed'.

Recalling JBCR

As the concepts behind the Classic Reading are woven into the fabric of each scene, we need only remember a scene to recall its truisms and, as the basic plot-line strings these scenes together, each scene serves as a memory jog for the next.

When we recall a scene, its embedded Classic Reading concepts are recalled with it

- We remember we are getting ready for a swanky party, indicating we can be sociable

- We remember planning our mission alone, indicating we can be introverted

- We remember locking up our secrets, indicating we can be wary

The plot strings the scenes together so we can recall Classic Reading concepts in sequence

- We know we are getting ready for the swanky party (the second scene in the plot), where we will be the centre of attention, which we enjoy...

Using JBCR

A character reading requires the Reader to say things to the Client in order to get a reaction. Recalling scenes (internally, to ourselves) from JBCR either in sequence, or at random, grants us access to a variety of truisms (riffs). Once verbalised to the Client as broad statements (riffing), these concepts can form the basis of a character reading.

To start a character reading, we recall the first scene from JBCR

- We remember we are getting ready for a swanky party, indicating we can be sociable

- We remember planning our mission alone, indicating we can be introverted

- We remember locking up our secrets, indicating we can be wary

We direct our conceptual riffs at the Client

> 'I'd imagine you can be sociable, but like downtime to do your own thing. I'm not saying you're an extrovert, but I'm

sure you've let your hair down on occasion. Your own personal projects do require that you spend time alone. You can be wary of people getting in the way of your plans, but need to find a balance between going out or staying in. I think you'd prefer it if you could be more consistent between your me time and fun time. You've learned not to trust everybody, but you can be fun to be around if you want to.'

- Once we have exhausted a scene's possibilities, the plot-line helps us remember the next scene

- We know we are getting ready for the swanky party (the second scene in the plot), where we will be the centre of attention, which we enjoy...

- We continue the reading until we feel the reading has lasted long enough, or it comes to its own natural conclusion.

Speed Learning JBCR

Although James Bond Cold Reading is easy to remember, you will learn quicker by approaching the material from different angles. The flash cards, audio and other support documentation for JBCR can certainly help in this regard, so be sure to download these from the website.

The flash cards serve as both a useful reference tool when starting out, and a handy refresher should you get rusty. Rather than being an exact transcript of this book, the audio elements comprise spaced repetition of JBCR to help stimulate the imagination, and to encourage you to forge detailed visualisations.

Here's some advice on how to learn JBCR as quickly as possible:

Stage One - Familiarisation

1. Read through the Classic Reading lines a few times, asking yourself how each line could apply to you.

2. Read through JBCR a few times, noting its broadened truisms.

3. Read through the JBCR plot and notice how it connects each script line with the next.

4. Repeat Stage One until you have a general understanding of the Classic Reading, the JBCR script, and its interconnecting plot.

Stage Two - Visualise

1. Read through and visualise each line of the JBCR script, making each scene as vivid as possible in your mind.

2. From memory, attempt to recall each scene from JBCR in sequence.

3. From memory, attempt to recall only the related truisms from each scene.

4. Repeat Stage Two until you can recall at least half of JBCR and its related truisms from memory.

Stage Three - Verbalise A

You may refer to the lines of the Classic Reading and JBCR during this stage

1. **Get Your Mouth In Gear,** and riff on each line of the Classic Reading until you run out of things to say.

2. **Get Your Mouth In Gear**, and riff on each line of JBCR until you run out of things to say.

3. Repeat this stage until you can riff for at least thirty seconds on each line or scene.

Stage Four - Verbalise B

This stage is to be practiced entirely from memory, no peeking allowed!

1. **Get Your Mouth In Gear**, and riff on each line of JBCR until you run out of things to say.

2. Make a note any problematic scenes, so you may strengthen the transition from their previous scenes.

3. Note any scene you feel could benefit from stronger visual ideas and hooks.

4. Repeat this stage until you feel more familiar with JBCR than the last time around and then...

5. Start again from Stage One

To keep things fresh while pushing yourself further, try doing these three simple things:

- Imagine how a friend or relative would react to your conceptual riffs

- Use as many synonyms as you can to describe each truism

- Allow transitions to inspire truisms of their own

If you know anything about Numerology (page 209), you can combine the meaning from each digit with the concept behind each JBCR line. For instance, the number one in Numerology signifies new beginnings, and you could incorporate this idea into a riff based on the first JBCR line 'You get ready alone...'

6

Oracular Vernacular

Now you understand the thinking behind James Bond Cold Reading, it's a good time to consider the many ways in which JBCR can be used. Cold Reading Games teaches how to give Palmistry, Graphology and Numerology readings, three traditional oracles that can be greatly enhanced using techniques found in JBCR. However, should you wish to forge your own path, you'll find non-traditional readings benefit greatly from the structures found in JBCR. This is particularly true of instances where you, the Reader, are anything but an expert in your chosen oracle.

Traditional Oracles With JBCR

Although James Bond Cold Reading can work as a stand-alone system, it works extremely well when combined with more traditional oracles in a variety of ways.

For example:

JBCR inspired riffs can be added ad-hoc to a traditional reading

> *Combining riffs derived from JBCR with traits derived from a traditional oracle is a simple and effective way to flesh-out a reading*

Traits uncovered during a traditional reading could trigger a riff that resembles a JBCR line

> *Should a trait remind you of a JBCR line, there's no harm in expanding on that trait using JBCR riffs you're familiar with*

Feedback from a Client during a traditional reading could invoke a JBCR riff

> *Should a Client mention a concept that reminds you of a JBCR line, you could develop that concept through a series of riffs.*

The sequence of your current system could invoke a similarly numbered JBCR line

> *The second line of the hand, the fifth letter in a sample of handwriting, or the number seven, could all invoke a corresponding line of JBCR.*

Non-Traditional Oracles With JBCR

Non-traditional oracles tend to be pseudo-scientific, and as such offer fewer mechanics with which to engage a Client. Client's won't believe their hair style alone grants an unimpeded insight into their psyche, so careful thought must be given to the implied method's procedure. An experience must be woven on which to hang one's remarkable abilities, or they simply won't be believed by a Client. To claim expertise in any skill, consideration must be made of the practical elements involved in performing that skill.

For example:

A body language expert needs time to observe a Client in order to form an opinion

> *You can't claim to read a Client's body language if they're motionless.*

An interrogation expert assesses a Client's answers during questioning

> *Aimless questions are not sufficient to convince a Client of your interrogation prowess.*

A sociology expert uses a Client's interactions with others to assess their character

> *A raft of Client insights can't possibly come from a single handshake and a smile.*

If you want to give non-traditional readings, you should be at least familiar with the procedures of your chosen oracle's skill-set. Put aside the time to study body language, FBI interrogation procedures, sociological profiling or anything else you feel important to your offering. You don't have to be a master of your field, but you do have to at least act and behave with a level of authority. Knowledge is power, so to avoid getting caught out by a real expert, do your research. Learn to use, or at least mimic, their techniques. You may feel that runes and tarot cards are passé, but you can't escape their theatrical appeal, nor the fact that Clients enjoy their modus operandi. If your oracular procedure is not similarly entertaining you will not only lose your Client's interest, but your own credibility as well.

Hot Or Not

A reading stops being cold when we use known facts about a Client to enhance a reading. Unless you are giving readings professionally to random strangers, it's rare to give any kind of reading which is not at least *slightly* warm to some extent.

As discussed, cold readings offer broad, one-size-fits-all statements that are interpreted as specific by the sitter. Hot Readings offer broad statements based on specific knowledge of a sitter, and the reader must judge the best distance from the facts to avoid unwanted scrutiny.

Let's use James Bond to give an example of a Hot Reading, before moving on to readings with a little less heat.

Hot Readings

James Bond wants your opinion. He wants to know what makes him tick, what makes him who he is. He wants a character reading, and has decided you're the person for the job. He doesn't know he's famous, but you've read the books and seen the films so, rather than a cold reading, you will be giving James Bond a Hot Reading.

Fictional characters such as James Bond are strong archetypes, and their behaviour and beliefs give us great examples of how many of us act and see the world. By taking two mental steps back from being in Bond's shoes, we can concoct phrases that can apply to almost anyone, yet resonate with Bond more than the generic truisms of the Classic Reading.

If you knew a person was James Bond, you could propose lines like:

- You have had your fair share of exciting times in the past
- You have to look out for yourself much of the time and be careful who you trust
- You like female attention but only when it suits you
- Sometimes you feel as if you are leading a double life
- There was someone in your past you wish you could have settled down with

Although the last line above is fairly broad regarding settling down, we know for a fact that Bond wed Teresa Draco in On Her Majesty's Secret Service, but tragedy intervened. Many people over a certain age wonder if they could have had a long-term relationship with a previous partner, but in Bond's case, and through no fault of his own, his bride died in the crossfire of an assassination attempt.

> **TOP TIP: Assassination attempts are the kind of prior knowledge that are entirely unsuitable as the basis for a truism, and should be avoided at all costs.**

Giving James Bond an imaginary reading is a useful way to generate truisms. Now let's apply this idea to other fictional characters.

GYMIG #1 - Hot Readings 👄

Imagine the following fictional characters are demanding a reading. By mentally distancing yourself from each character's truth, see how much you can tell them about themselves. How vague can you go while remaining relevant, and how close to the facts can you get without sounding like a stalker?

Harry Potter	**The Hulk**	**Charlie Brown**
Captain Kirk	**Lara Croft**	**Indiana Jones**
Bilbo Baggins	**Homer Simpson**	

If you find it difficult at first, try going from the specific to the general. Here's an example using Bilbo Baggins:

- You once wore a ring without realising it was the One Ring of The Dark Lord Sauron
- You once found a ring whose evil power drove you to the brink of sanity
- There is something in your history that you still yearn for from time to time
- You can make plans and think ahead, but have a tendency to dwell on the past

Using fictional characters to generate truisms is a useful tool, and just the thought of one can help you get unstuck during a reading. The added quirks of fictitious characters can keep things fresh, and can help keep your banter far enough from the facts to remain relevant. Vanilla characters who speak for us all work best for this exercise, so Bond villains, serial killers and anti-heroes are out. With a bit of practice, you'll find yourself jumping from the specific to the general without breaking a sweat.

> **TOP TIP:** You should never be afraid of taking your time when giving a reading. It is not a race, so pace things accordingly. A few seconds absorbed in a mind game never hurt anyone, so allow yourself time to think. Remember, no Client wants a reading that feels rushed, and readings work best at the pace of a ticking grandfather clock.

Fictional Stereotypes

My friends and I have a game we play while socialising called the Lookalike Game, that begins when one of us calls out a celebrity's name. It soon becomes clear that, rather than actual star-spotting, we're in search of a famous doppelgänger. After confirming the identity of the lookalike (and arguing whether they look alike at all) the game pauses until a new celebrity is named and the search starts anew.

As more celebrities are named, the available choices dwindle, making it progressively harder to choose and identify lookalikes. It gets to where any moustache makes someone a Freddy Mercury, and the faintest sight of hair dye casts them as Lady Gaga. The more vague the similarities the sillier the game gets, and attempts to keep the whole thing a secret, especially in public, make it hard to keep a straight face.

Fun and games aside, stereotyping can help generate truisms, and approaching Clients as if they were their famous doppelgänger can be a useful tool. As long as you take several steps back from the fictional character's traits, you can ensure your riffs are broad enough to sound insightful. Unlike the lookalike game, you will come up with truisms through the lens of the characters they play. You will be riffing on Bond, not Connery and, should you meet his lookalike too, Harry Potter rather than Radcliffe.

GYMIG #2 - Fictional Stereotypes 👄

Pull up a random image of a stranger from the internet / social media and, similar to The Lookalike Game, jump to the idea of a fictional character from your initial reaction to their image. It could be their hair, eyes, clothing, even the way they look at the camera. Then, imagining this stranger is sitting in front of you, come up with truisms for them based on the fictional character you have in mind. You will have no choice but to talk in broad strokes or your imaginary sitter will find you out. Suggesting that a Hulk lookalike turns green when angry is pointless, whereas asking if they feel frustrated, or whether they harbour untapped inner potential, makes perfect sense.

Friends And Family Stereotypes

Taking Fictional Stereotypes a step further, creating truisms on the fly is relatively easy when reading for people who resemble a close friend or relation. For instance, you might meet a guy called Peter who, for whatever reason, reminds you of your cousin Paul. You already know Paul well, so you could do worse than riff in broad terms to Peter on concepts relating to Paul.

> **TOP TIP: A Client that reminds you of Charlie Brown does not mean they have a dog, or that they even like dogs. Keep several steps back and you won't get bitten.**

GYMIG #3 - Friends And Family Stereotypes

Pull up a random image of a stranger from the internet / social media and use anything you can about the person's image to link them to one of your friends or close acquaintances. Don't overthink it, find something that connects the person's image to a person you know. If you're stuck, take a stab at their age and pick someone you know of a similar age. Then, imagining this stranger is sitting in front of you, come up with truisms for them based on your friend or acquaintance.

Let's not forget that readings using stereotypes are tools to help create broad statements similar to those found in the Classic Reading. Although someone may remind you of a friend, celebrity of fictional character, you need to riff several steps back from the original stereotype, deconstructing from the specific to the broad. A Client need never know they reminded you of Tony Soprano or Cruella De Ville and, if they are anything like them, it's best kept that way.

Tepid Readings

Would a reading from a tarot card reader at a busy psychic fair be as cold as one given to someone straight off the street? Possibly, but highly unlikely.

As a thought exercise, let's imagine you have been hired to give cold readings at two events. Billed as 'The People Reader', you are not expected to do anything at these events but tell people about themselves to their faces, completely cold, without relying on any kind of oracle such as Palmistry.

One event is a team-building event for Meta, the umbrella company for Facebook, Instagram and WhatsApp. The other is a launch party for Metallica's new album.

There's no doubt you'd approach both the Meta and Metallica events with a different mindset. Knowing a group's demographic gives you a head-start, and within a few minutes of mingling with either crowd, you would get a feel for how they talk, act and relate to each other before any reading occurred. Although a reading given immediately on arrival at either event would be tepid at most, a reading given after twenty minutes of simple observation would be a lot warmer.

Warm Readings

None of us live in a vacuum, and that is why most readings tend to be, at the very least, warm.

Let's imagine that, at the Meta event, you have a brief chat with Corporate Geoff, who admits he loves Metallica. Corporate Geoff is head of data sprockets at Meta and, like most people at the event, looks nothing like your stereotypical metal fan. As this is a paid gig and you cannot be seen talking idly to the guests, you give Corporate Geoff your best 'People Reader' stare and begin telling him about himself.

Now, you're not going into Corporate Geoff's reading cold for at least two reasons. One, you know he works for Meta and is head of data sprockets, and two, you also know he loves Metallica. Knowing what someone is passionate about can be incredibly insightful, especially when these passions appear at odds with their appearance. Corporate Geoff looks the part at the Meta event, yet he likes Metallica and possibly lots of other rock music. Compared to his work colleagues, is Corporate Geoff slightly different? If so, do you think he has faced any challenges on his rise to fame at Meta?

Perhaps some of these lines would resonate with Corporate Geoff:

- You have a different outlook from some of your work colleagues
- You are comfortable working with people from different backgrounds
- Although you work in a corporate environment, you have never lost your individuality

Now let's imagine we meet Rock Geoff at the Metallica event. Rock Geoff is wearing a Metallica t-shirt, has long hair and looks at home back-stage at a rock gig. Rock Geoff admits, after a brief conversation, that he is head of data sprockets at Meta. It's the same Geoff, of course, and the clash of his Meta-Metallica persona is as insightful as before.

Perhaps some of these lines would resonate with Rock Geoff:

- You have a different outlook from some of your rock friends
- You are comfortable making friends with people from different backgrounds
- Although you love music, you have stayed focused on your software career

Apart from changing things up to match the setting, both of Geoff's stories are the same.

Specific information regarding a sitter's cultural taste can be used to your advantage should you be sufficiently knowledgeable in music, film, or any other art form. For instance, if you knew that Stuart's favourite music was ambient techno, Jane's favourite film genre was slasher horror, and Patrick was a big fan of Renaissance portraiture, you'd have an inkling into how each of them viewed the world. If you knew specifically that Stuart's favourite musical artist was Aphex Twin, Jane's favourite film was The Ring and Patrick's favourite contemporary artist was Anish Kapoor, you'd have even more to go on.

However, we can break these stereotypes by imagining that techno-loving Stuart is in his eighties, horror-movie Jane runs a creche, and art-buff Patrick drives trucks for a living. As with Geoff, the metal loving data expert, these Broken Stereotypes give you far more food for thought than their vanilla counterparts. People are multi-faceted, and you can get a lot of mileage using truisms that bridge the gap between the vastly different aspects of people's personalities.

GYMIG #4 - Broken Stereotypes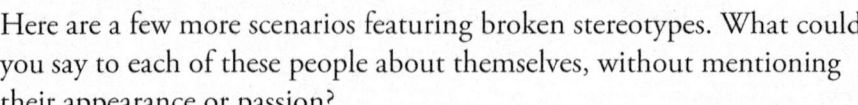

Here are a few more scenarios featuring broken stereotypes. What could you say to each of these people about themselves, without mentioning their appearance or passion?

- A young woman in a loud floral dress (whose favourite TV show is The X Files)
- A male, thirty-something leather-clad biker (whose guilty pleasure is Celine Dion)
- A suited and booted middle-aged man (who loves anime, with a soft spot for Dragon Ball Z)

Hot Readings Revisited

Hot Readings can be a double-edged sword.

When we gave a Hot Reading to James Bond, he had no idea he was famous, and had no chance of backtracking our method, no matter how close we came to the truth. In the real world, a Hot Reading requires at least some specific knowledge of a sitter beforehand, and for obvious reasons, this will work better with people you know something about, rather than people you know well.

For instance, you give a reading to Vicky from accounts at your works Christmas party. You've not met Vicky in person, but have noticed several of your work-colleagues sharing her Instagram account online, which mainly revolves around her passion for Taekwondo and her love of Formula One. Interesting stuff, but you need to tread lightly to ensure Vicky cannot backtrack anything you say about her via the workplace. Telling her she punched above her weight, or lived life in the fast lane, would be a dead giveaway, but describing her as a strong, focused, and thrill-seeking individual could help colour your truisms with a hint of personality. Pastel shaded truths, rather than poster-painted facts, are the order of the day here.

Hot Reading brings with it a host of moral ambiguities, so it's best to avoid mentioning anything that could trigger a negative response from a Client. By all means base truisms on the fact that Mary got married or Kevin aced his driving test, but avoid Marion's messy divorce and Kelvin's road-rage incident. If you are aware of only negative things regarding a person, it's best to feign ignorance by giving them a broad, positive and upbeat reading, rather than treading areas best left well alone. Hot Readings should feel slightly more insightful to a Client than a cold reading, but no more than that, as Clients deserve empathy rather than revelations. Clients know what they do in their lives, and there's no point telling them they recently fixed a puncture or burnt a casserole. If you get too close to the mundane truth, you may well end up being burnt at the Hot Reading stake.

> **TOP TIP: Hot Readings can be tricky to navigate, so be cautious at first. It's easy to jump to conclusions through the lenses of our own beliefs and prejudices, so use prior knowledge of a Client sparingly, if at all.**

White Hot Readings

The hottest and most useless of readings, White Hot Readings are dead in the water. It's almost impossible to impress friends and acquaintances as we already know them and broad, sweeping statements about their personal lives sound obviously phoney. Truisms forged many steps back from the facts are easily traceable, and attempts to appear insightful can appear both transparent, and ridiculous. To quote the comedian Harry Hill, "You can tell a lot about people... by what they're like."

To give readings to friends, you need to shift the focus away from your own abilities as a 'People Reader' to some kind of oracle, such as Palmistry. Oracular systems are vague and open to interpretation, bursting at the seams with broad, generalised descriptors, and are the world's original truism generators. However, with the focus on a system, you will find most friends and relations, no matter how cynical, will be happy to delve into a traditional reading. The oracle holds the secret, and you are simply the messenger. The heat is off.

A Catalogue Of Truisms

Creating a catalogue of truisms is both a beneficial exercise, and a useful tool. You can seek inspiration by browsing daily horoscopes, but it's worth concocting your own lines.

Here's a quick way of getting your catalogue started, based on the ideas outlined in this chapter:

- Write down as many truisms as you can that could apply to James Bond.

- Apply the same technique to several other fictional characters of your choice.

- Do the same for people you know well; parents, friends, acquaintances and work colleagues.

- Compare every trait, looking specifically for lines you feel could apply to anyone.

- Do what works best for you, and keep refining and adding to your catalogue of truisms. A simple exercise book works just fine, but using a spreadsheet or mind-map to cross reference your entries can be illuminating.

> **TOP TIP:** You can learn a huge amount about Cold Reading from traditional oracles. Forer's experiment shone a light on a cold reading principle that existed centuries before the publication of the first horoscope.

7

Shaping a Reading

Although it's possible to deliver a character reading via a series of James Bond Cold Reading riffs, the last thing we want is to lose the Client in a directionless train of thought. A reading is a narrative and requires a sense of progression to keep our Client's informed, entertained, and coming back for more. It turns out that a great template for this kind of narrative is the tried and tested Bond film itself.

Most, if not all, Bond films deliver an enthralling, progressive and climactic story, and their stylised titles and end credits are legendary. Tales of espionage may keep us entertained, but the titles set the tone, and the credits give us the chance to talk over the theme song as we discuss the film's best (and worst) bits.

Likewise, readings flow better with some kind of Three Act Structure. Similar to the titles and credits of a Bond film, an Introduction can help set the tone of the reading, and a Summary can highlight a reading's best bits (whilst ignoring the worst).

Introduction (Titles)

Before a reading starts, you should say a few words about your chosen oracle. A brief introduction on how you came to practice traditional Palmistry, or a potted history of Numerology, can help a Client relax and settle in. With less traditional oracles, such as claiming you are a forensics expert, you may need to concoct a more elaborate spiel.

Regardless of your opening gambit, you would do well to infuse your introduction with these two very important ideas:

1. **Diffuse any concept that the reading is a challenge**

   By requesting help, openness and honesty from your Client to ensure the reading's success, the idea that the reading is some kind of challenge is diminished.

2. **Share responsibility for the reading with the spectator**

   Emphasis should be placed firmly on the idea that the reading is a cooperative process requiring both Reader, and Client, to work together towards a positive outcome.

A joint effort approach helps negate the thought of failure, and the idea that readings are a process rather than an outcome can put the Client in a suitably inquisitive mindset. You should be helping each other explore possibilities, not closing down mutual avenues of interest.

Summary (Credits)

Summaries are an important tool in their own right, from which all readings can benefit. During the summary, we get the chance to highlight and expand on our successful riffs whilst ignoring lesser riffs wholesale. Our brief and optimistic re-telling of the reading will be the last thing the Client hears and, by simple reinforcement, will make up the bulk of anything they remember.

The summary also indicates that the reading is winding down, and can help draw a line under readings that have overstayed their welcome for either party. Clients that come specifically for a reading have a habit of losing track of time, whereas the occasional impromptu, yet nervy, Client can find even the shortest of readings long and tortuous. Whether a Client looks uncomfortable, a reading turns sour, or you are running ten minutes over schedule, the summary is a way out for the Reader and / or the Client. Lesser readings can be salvaged, and good readings can be re-forged for the better during a summary, so never end a reading without one.

THREE ACT STRUCTURE

As discussed, JBCR is largely an exercise in extemporisation, but we'd all like a reading that builds to a high before the end credits of the summary. To this end, we need some kind of structure.

Some traditional oracles have structure built-in, such as the three card Tarot reading signifying past, present and future. This beginning, middle and end structure mirrors the three act dramatic structure found in most fictional narrative. As people are more interested in their future than their past, three card readings build to an exciting yet mysterious final act by design.

LENSES OF TIME

An important concept defining three card Tarot readings is that each card is perceived through a different Lens Of Time. Asking the Client to reflect on each card through a different lens mimics, to some extent, the trials and tribulations faced by the fictional character Scrooge in 'A Christmas Carol' by Charles Dickens. Invited by Marley's ghost to witness (and interpret) Christmas past, present and future in turn, Scrooge changes his nature (and therefore his future) for the better. Reinforcing the notion of self-determination is essential during a reading, so it's worth bearing in mind that, if someone as dreadful as Ebenezer Scrooge can learn a lesson, so too can your Client.

The first card in a three card tarot reading is viewed through the Lens Of Past. As the past is a very long time indeed, it's almost impossible for a Client to not see at least *something* of themselves represented in this card. The second card is viewed through the Lens Of Present, a malleable lens that can stretch back several years to accommodate what the Client deems recent. The third card is viewed through the Lens Of Future, and invites the Client to compare the symbolism on the card with their hopes, aspirations, and dreams for the future. These hopes could well have been touched upon before the third card is dealt, but will always be grounded in the Client's personal reality. Rather than moon landings and Nobel prizes, most people's expectations are rooted in the mundanity of everyday life, and mainly concern relationships, pay rises, and career prospects.

Past, Recent Past And Present

To help give our JBCR reading a sense of progression, we can adopt a similar three act structure to our reading, observing our riffs through each lens in turn. We can do this internally or externally, either wording our riffs with no mention of the current lens in mind, or by telling a Client specifically when we are moving from one act, or lens, to the next. The first two acts work similarly to Tarot readings, each riff opening with a phrase that describes the lens through which it is to be viewed.

It should be noted that lenses are relative to age, and you will find an eighteen-year-old's concept of the recent past differ drastically from someone approaching their seventieth birthday. It's important to adjust your timescale, and therefore your riffs, accordingly.

Here are some examples of how to open a riff using the lenses of past, recent past and present:

Act One: Lens Of Past (many years ago)

- When you were much younger, I get the feeling that...

- When you were growing up, you may have...

- During your teens, you had a propensity to...

- As you matured, you probably felt a need to...

Act Two: Lens Of Present (and recent past)

- For the last year or two, you may have been feeling...

- Leading up to this moment, I get the sense that...

- Nowadays I get the impression that you're...

- Currently I get the feeling that you are ready for...

Notice that each act has within it a progression of its own, from childhood to adolescence in Act One, and from the last few years up to the present moment in Act Two. It's often best to riff from soft-focus (sometime in the past, 'when you were younger') to sharp-focus (specific to an era, 'as a child') and to adjust your focus according to your Client's responses.

These example openings will not fit every JBCR scene, but can give you some indication of the tone to aim for. In practice, you will be selecting scenes internally before verbalising them through either lens, allowing you a few moments to think of a suitable way to open your riff.

The Future

The lenses of past and present work similarly to those used in Tarot readings. The Third Act, however, works differently, as we need to riff on ideas based solely on what we believe to be the character of the Client. By re-framing a reading's more successful riffs through the lens of future, we can create new riffs encouraging the Client to trust and nurture any **Strength Of Character** (SOC) they possess, to help overcome life's challenges. For instance, you may have discovered during a reading that the Client is good under pressure, and is trustworthy, patient and kind. It is these Strengths Of Character you must riff on, to project a third and final act that looks to the future.

Here are some examples of how to open a riff using the lens of future:

Act Three: Lens Of Future

- Moving forward, I can see you using your SOC to...

- Thinking of the future, you could do well to use your SOC to...

- Whatever the future holds, there is a good chance your SOC will help you overcome...

- With your SOC and SOC, you will find yourself able to cope with those challenges that...

As the riffs of Act Three are derived from the most successful riffs of Act One and Act Two, there's a good chance you will know a fair bit about the Client by this point. However, while some Clients are an open book, others may give nothing away, and you may have little choice but to skip to the summary sooner than intended.

When using the Lens Of Future, it's important to praise your Client's Strengths Of Character rather than conjuring possibilities from thin air, as predicting positive or negative outcomes for enterprises beyond human knowledge can be harmful. Fanning the flames of fantasy may make the Client feel good, but there is a strong chance that they (and possibly you) may get burnt when things do not work out. It's fine to discuss choices and outcomes based on personal strengths, but don't fall into the trap of making predictions you think the Client wants to hear.

Get Your Mouth In Gear #1 - 3

1. Riff on any scene of JBCR through the lens of past
2. Riff on any scene of JBCR through the lens of present / recent past
3. Riff on any scene of JBCR through the lens of future

Retrospective Lenses

A lens can be used at any time to re-frame a riff that falls flat. The idea is that, should a riff get less than a positive reaction, the riff is re-imagined through a different lens with help from the Client. The easiest way to illustrate this is with some terrible cold reading blunders, saved in part by a quick re-frame through the lenses of past, present and future.

- Karen looks uncertain when you tell her she has a tendency to be pessimistic. You tell her you sensed pessimism from something in her recent past, although you are not sure of the context exactly. Can she help explain this discrepancy?

- David does not warm to the idea that he likes to travel. You appear confused and explain that you sense that may change in the future, and ask if there is a foreign culture he finds particularly interesting.

- Mary does not look convinced when you tell her she can be

stubborn. You explain how this feeling may derive from her earlier years, and ask if she sometimes still feels like a teenager.

If you are not using three act structure, you can re-frame an unsuccessful riff through any lens you like but, if you are using three acts, you can suggest you mistook one lens for another i.e. mistook a future riff for a past riff. Suggesting that the timeline is the problem, rather than the riff itself, invites the Client to get involved in helping make sense of your statement. You'd be surprised how many bad riffs can lead to extremely interesting conversations, once they are kicked into a different timeline.

Get Your Mouth In Gear #4

4. Pick a random line from JBCR and, imagining a negative response from the Client, reframe its meaning through the lens of past or future via a series of riffs. Not all lines are as malleable as each other, so try this with several lines, and take note of those you find difficult to reimagine.

Topical Lenses - CHARM School

As I mentioned earlier, the concerns of most people are predictable and mundane. Some of us are curious about our careers and, at a certain age, wonder whether our health will remain good enough for us to do the things we want to do. We'd all like our ambitions to amount to something, would be happy for some romance once in a while, and could all do with a little more money.

James Bond has **CHARM** in abundance and it turns out that the five topical lenses of Career, Health, Ambition, Romance and Money are just as useful as those relating to time. These lenses are sensitive to the life-stage of the Client but, generally speaking, you can use these lenses at any point during a reading. At least one of these five topics will concern a Client at any one time so, if you use each of the CHARM lenses during a reading, you are almost sure to hit a nerve at some point.

As an example, here is Scene 3 from JBCR seen through each of the five topical lenses in turn:

#1 Lens Of Career

Although cool and confident, you are nervous about the mission.

> *'Working out which steps to take next in your career have given you some sleepless nights, but your work colleagues would never know it as you are able to play your cards quite close to your chest.'*

Retirees are less concerned about their careers than people in their twenties, but retirement can be a dirty word to an entrepreneur.

#2 Lens Of Health

Although cool and confident, you are nervous about the mission.

> *'We all worry about our health to some degree or other, but being open about your health concerns is better for everyone.'*

No matter how young a Client appears, either physically or mentally, their true state of health is unknown to us, and possibly unknown to them.

#3 Lens Of Ambition

Although cool and confident, you are nervous about the mission.

> *'I get the impression that you often feel you are winging it and, although you know you have what it takes to achieve your goals, you are often your own worst enemy.'*

Ambition doesn't dwindle, but can shift as priorities change in a person's life. Personal ambition can often take a back seat to the collective ambition of rearing a healthy family.

#4 Lens Of Romance

Although cool and confident, you are nervous about the mission.

> *'Matters of the heart can take their toll, but you have learned to keep your composure through thick and thin.'*

Romance can fizzle out when people settle down, but older adults can yearn for affection as much as anyone–especially those that outlive their partner.

#5 Lens Of Money

Although cool and confident, you are nervous about the mission.

> *'You may give the impression that money is not an issue to you, but sometimes it worries you more than you'd like to admit.'*

Money affords us our current lifestyle, and most people's money worries concern financial security, and socio-economic status.

The Lens Of Health should be flagged here as it is not only the lens most susceptible to a Client's age, it is the most risky to discuss. On the whole, young adults do not give their health a second thought, but there are always those who have had a childhood full of health problems.

Likewise, most Clients approaching middle-age are perfectly healthy, but some feel their bones creaking sooner than others. One thing you can count on is that health, both mentally and physically, is of increasing concern for the middle-aged and beyond.

Be mindful of being dragged into questions pertaining to a Client's health and, should you feel uncomfortable, politely decline any further conversation on the topic. Don't be afraid to suggest the Client seek (or continue) professional medical help.

> **Get Your Mouth In Gear #5**
>
> 5. Riff on a random line from JBCR using any lens from the CHARM acronym. Repeat the process as many times as you like, taking special note of the difficulties that can arise when using the lens of health.

INNER AND OUTER LENSES

Our inner world of hopes and dreams can often differ from the outward practicalities of our day-to-day lives. The way we feel about things internally is not always mirrored by our external actions, and we often put on a brave face to mitigate our doubts and insecurities. Internal struggles are often harder to overcome than external forces, and no compelling protagonist was ever written without a good blend of the two. James Bond would be a simple action hero were it not for his inner struggle, and a good Bond story uses the tension between his personal needs, and the needs of the state, to keep us engaged.

Like Retrospective Lenses, one of the best uses of inner and outer lenses is to reframe traits that illicit a mixed response from the Client. A trait can be reimagined as either pertaining more to a Client's internal world of thoughts and feelings or their external world of action and commitment. One is mental, the other physical.

Here are some traits seen through both lenses, followed by examples:

Trait	Inner Lens	Outer Lens
Energetic	Full of thoughts	Full of beans
Romantic	Hides secret crushes	Heart on their sleeve
Creative	Personal projects	Collaborative works

Energetic

- Outer To Inner Lens - *'You may not think of yourself as active, but your mind never sits still.'*

- Inner To Outer Lens - *'Rather than overthinking things, you like to make things happen.'*

Romantic

- Outer To Inner Lens - *'Do you find it hard to be open with your feelings? You could be a romantic introvert.'*

- Inner To Outer Lens - *'Rather than keeping things bottled up inside, you could be the more flirtatious type.'*

Creative

- Outer To Inner Lens - *'Your creativity may not be obvious to those around you, but it helps keep you sane.'*

- Inner To Outer Lens - *'Maybe you are less reclusive and more big picture. You are about possibilities.'*

You will not always be reframing from one extreme to the other, but it's a useful and memorable way of thinking about these lenses.

Get Your Mouth In Gear #6 - 7

6. Riff on any line from JBCR through the inner lens.
7. Riff on any line from JBCR through the outer lens.

STRUCTURE IN A STRUCTURE

The twelve scene structure of JBCR is such that it lends itself easily to three acts, each comprising four scenes. Should you wish, you could riff on the first four scenes through the lens of past, the middle four scenes through the lens of present, and the last four scenes through the lens of future. For a shorter reading, you could cut it down to two scenes per lens, or just the one if you're pushed for time.

Although we can use the acronym CHARM to remember the topical lenses, it's easy to use the concepts embedded in each scene of JBCR as a reminder of their existence.

- The swanky party in scene one can remind us of Money.

- Hoping the mission goes well in scene four can remind us of Ambition.

- Our sexual side in scene seven can remind us of Romance.

- Wondering about our choice to be a spy in scene nine can remind us of Career

- Dr No is a doctor, although not the best for Bond's Health.

Although CHARM covers the topics most people are concerned about, we can view our riffs through any lens we see fit, and embed these topics into any scene. A visualisation of Bond tipping a waiter at the party could remind us of the money lens, an extra photo of a loved one in Bond's wallet can remind us to mention family, and escaping on a plane can remind us to use the lens of travel. Compile a list of your own topical lenses, and experiment with creating lenses on the fly. These can be wide and overarching, such as mind, body and spirit, or more specific, like parents and pets. If a spontaneous new idea or theme pops up when running through a JBCR scene, try using it as a lens.

Get Your Mouth In Gear #8

8. Visualise each scene of JBCR in your mind, taking note not only of anything that reminds you of a lens, but of objects, places, people and feelings that could act as new lenses. As you do this, describe what you see by speaking out loud.

Lens Within A Lens

Looking through several lenses at once is almost unavoidable, and that's not a bad thing. Viewing a JBCR line through the lenses of past and of money will give you a dramatically different riff to that of a line viewed through the lenses of future and romance. Throw the inner and outer lenses into the mix and the possibilities increase even further. How about a JBCR line viewed through the ambition, past and inner lenses, then reimagined through the career, future and outer lenses?

Lenses are supremely powerful and can help breathe life into the most lacklustre of traits. Try mixing them up, and don't be afraid to invent your own!

Get Your Mouth In Gear #9

9. Riff on a random JBCR line through three lenses at the same time; the lens of time, a topical lens and an inner or outer lens. Do this several times, and be mindful of any riff you feel oversteps the mark by either being too specific, or too personal. As always, take special care with the health lens and, if it makes you feel uncomfortable, avoid it all together.

For more ideas on getting a reading going, read the opening few pages of the Palmistry section page 118.

8

Lucky Escapes

It's Bond's close-shaves that keep us entertained, and a Bond film where everything goes to plan would be boring. The same applies to readings as, devoid of friction, a reading can feel dull and lifeless. Encouraging mistakes keeps us on our toes, fosters creativity, and gives our readings an edge. Better to be adventurous like Bond, than play it safe and bore The Living Daylights out of everyone.

Using contradictions as a tool is a concept I have stressed throughout my work on giving readings. The idea is that friction, rather than something to be avoided, is the seam where the gold lies. Inconsistencies in a reading can jolt a Client into conversation, and this feedback can help you tailor the narrative accordingly.

Traditional Reading Waypoints

During a Traditional Reading, friction comes from the oracle itself. This friction is detached from the opinions of those involved, as it's plain to see on the hand, in a Client's handwriting or number chart. Rather than avoiding these mis-steps at all costs, highlight them as waypoints, and make a note to revisit them once you've learnt more about the Client. With these waypoints in mind, you can explore signs later in the reading that point in the same direction, either by luck or reinterpretation.

For instance:

- You discover two conflicting Palmistry traits on a Client's hand. You explain to the Client that you should both bear this conflict in mind, and seek out any answers that may shed light on these conflicts as the reading progresses.

- While studying a Client's handwriting, you note their cursive handwriting is at odds with their signature. You explain that further analysis may uncover the truth behind this discrepancy.

- A Client finds the number meanings encountered near the start of a Numerology reading somewhat contradictory. You make a note to return to these ideas, once you've got more numbers to work with.

> For more thoughts on contradictions, see the Seams Of Gold section on page 139.

James Bond Cold Reading Waypoints

During James Bond Cold Reading, and other truism based readings such as the Classic Reading, friction is generated when a Client simply disagrees with what you've said about them. With no oracle to fall back on (or to blame), your comments are exposed and your hunch is wrong. It's your word against theirs, and the Client knows themselves a lot better than you do.

The best way to approach this scenario is to acknowledge your inaccuracies up front, and pledge to understand what you meant when you said what you said. More importantly still, you need to request the Client's help in doing this. If a Client does nothing more than shake their head in disagreement, ask them why, and explain that their input is a valuable and important part of the reading experience.

Here are some examples of potential mis-steps that could occur during a reading. What could you say to these people to turn the tide in your favour?

- You tell Mary she has found it unwise to be too frank in revealing herself to others, but she shakes her head in disagreement whilst describing herself as an open book.

- When told she prefers a certain amount of change and variety, Steph looks wary and confesses to being a rather anxious individual, who dislikes change and hates surprises.

- A riff based on the Classic Reading line 'some of your aspirations tend to be pretty unrealistic' gets a negative reaction from a Client called Brian, who sees himself as a practical, hardworking pillar of society.

Let's take a look at what we could say to Mary, Steph and Brian:

- **Mary** - *'That's really interesting, an open book you say? Well, that's going to make this reading easy for me, isn't it? I wonder why I was picking up on some kind of shyness. Perhaps with your help we can discover why I said that. Thanks for being honest with me. It really helps me get better at what I do.'*

- **Steph** - *'Well, that is surprising! I was sensing the word change for some reason. Do you know why that is? No? Well, let's come back to it if we find any clues along the way. Be sure to pick me up on any other things I say that don't fully resonate with you, ok?'*

- **Brian** - *'Yes, I can really see that now, actually. I was sensing something about aspirations, aspirational perhaps? You're probably an inspiration to a lot of people. Am I right? Perhaps it's unrealistic to think you can help all the people who look up to you. Thanks for setting me straight and stay on my case, it's the only way I can get better at this.'*

It's important to note that, in order to disagree with you, each Client has had to tell you why. Mary thinks of herself as an open book, Steph has admitted to being worrisome, and Brian is rather full of himself. This is all valuable information that can help guide your reading. Knowing Mary is an open book means you can conduct the rest of her reading safe in the knowledge she will be chatty, approachable and open to debate. The worrisome Steph may be quite the opposite, and her reading is likely to be a more insular affair focusing on her inner world and her fears, hopes and anxieties. And the somewhat egotistical Brian sounds like he will be happy whenever you are stroking his ego, or pandering to his overblown sense of importance.

Nothing creates as much conversation as a gentle disagreement, so you need to learn to embrace these moments of friction and dare to be less than right. A minor adjustment is usually all that is required as, due to its improvisational nature, chatter generated by JBCR tends to be broad and open to debate.

Shifting Focus

You will notice that to soften the blow of being wrong in Steph and Brian's readings, I went back and focused on just one word, *change* with Steph, and *aspirations* with Brian. Asking the Client to interpret just one word of a **False Trait** takes the heat off, and gives them something to focus on while you plan your next move. Finding meaning in a single word can be quite a challenge, but as a thought-exercise for the Client it has the potential to take the reading in a new direction, whilst eclipsing any memory of your original inaccuracy.

> You can learn more about False Traits on page 143.

The Humble Vessel

Another useful tactic is to think of your riffs as separate from yourself, objects ripe for interpretation that even you may not understand. In Brian's scenario, I tried to understand what I meant; did I mean inspirational, or aspirational, and who am I to truly understand what falls from my lips? Sometimes it helps to think of your mouth as an oracle you have little control over, one that creates verbal insights ripe for interpretation, wholly separate from yourself and the Client. You may be riffing on truisms plucked from JBCR, but can act as if you had no idea where they came from, or how to interpret them.

Bare Faced Flattery

Nothing gets you out of a tight spot faster than flattery, so praise the Client when hitting these waypoints. Brian disagreed strongly that his aspirations were unrealistic, so I told him I meant he's an inspiration to others. If you can connect the flattery to a recent riff, so much the better, but if you can't, it's best to say something so nice it doesn't matter. Judicious use of compliments can oil the wheels of a reading such that even the biggest gaffes zoom past, lost in the dust of flattery.

Breaking Serve

At the start of the conversation, Margaret shakes her head and says she never gets time alone, but I immediately reply with 'But you can be wary of people getting in the way of your plans, can't you?'. This is a patently obvious statement, as someone with no time alone will always be wary of people getting in the way of their plans. To derail her negative take on my first riff, I volleyed a version of her reply back to her. This made it appear I had not finished talking, and that her sentiment was where my initial riff was headed.

Other Techniques

The Truth Train

Riffs that ring true for the Client, especially those that get them talking, should be jumped upon. For instance, a Client could respond positively to the line 'You tend to dwell on the past a little too much sometimes...' and divulge that they recently split up with a partner. You could follow this immediately with '...yes, and I get the feeling you've found it hard being alone again.' Continuing your train of thought helps give the impression you were alluding to the Client's relationship all along. There's a knack to keeping this kind of dialogue in motion, but once it gets going, it can often span several riffs. The trick is to see how long you can stay onboard.

Divide And Conquer

An old marketing technique is to hijack negative responses by asking people which of two different versions of a product they prefer. With the chance of a yes / no answer off the table, potential customers are thrown into an imaginary scenario where the product, and their choices, matter. For instance, I know you're not in the market for one now, but if you *were* to buy a sprocket from us, would you go for the red one, or the blue one? You can use the same concept when giving readings.

- *'There's an air of vulnerability about you. Would that be on the inside, or the outside?'*

- *'You look like an idealist, but I'm not sure if that's a personal outlook, or your worldly outlook.'*

- *'I'm getting a sense that you like games. Would that be physical or mental?'*

Pick And Mix

This is the smorgasbord version of Divide And Conquer. Clients invariably home in on traits that interest them most whilst leaving other offerings behind so, rather than asking the Client to choose one of two versions of a trait, we offer a string of traits and await a response.

- *'There's an air of vulnerability about you. You look like an idealist, and I'm getting a sense you like games...'*

Any one of these traits could ring true for a Client. Once they have shown an interest in one you could, if you wish, use Divide And Conquer to give them a further two options as before.

- *'Yes, but when I say idealist, I'm not sure if that's a personal outlook or a world outlook.'*

Charm Offensive

Both Divide And Conquer and Pick And Mix can be combined with the CHARM method, to reveal the life topics that concern the Client. For instance, rather than asking flat-out whether a Client is more concerned with Romance rather than Money, we could say something like:

- *'I get the feeling you're a romantic at heart, but you're still able to focus on the money when needs be. I'm not sure how you balance these two aspects of your personality, but one side has taken a back seat lately. Does that make any sense?'*

In this example, I'm asking the Client to divulge the topic they're least interested in. This is a useful tactic, and prevents the more interesting topic being mentioned twice. For instance, if you learn that romance has taken a back seat, you can segue into the topic of money later. This is far less obvious than going straight into a riff based on a topic the Client seems most interested in.

Riffing It All Together

The examples above have all been fairly simplistic to get their points across. In use, you should riff on these ideas freely to create a broader, more colourful, dialogue:

> *'When it comes to relationships, you're either all in, or you're literally out of there. You can be an open book when you want to be, but you reserve your innermost secrets to only your closest of friends. You don't admit to being the best when it comes to juggling finances, but you're able to keep things going even during the hardest of times. You don't like to ask for help, as you have an independent streak, but you do have people you can rely on. These various aspects of your personality are intertwined somehow, but I can't quite make it out. Does anything I've said ring true for you at the present time?'*

Should a Client be unconcerned with the topics you are proposing, there's a good chance they will pick up on something else entirely. In the example above, they might home in on a problem with a close friendship rather than romance, or professional independence rather than financial. If it keeps the conversation flowing, it's all good, and you can revisit your CHARM offensive later with some different topics should you wish.

9

Protaganother

If you want to branch off in a new direction, try shifting your focus to a different protagonist such as Lara Croft from Tomb Raider, or Tyrion Lannister from Game Of Thrones. With a little thought, you can attach a different set of cold reading lines to these characters, and use them in tandem with James Bond Cold Reading. The principles of JBCR can work with any character you know well, so don't be afraid to reframe the Classic Reading into a character or genre you are familiar with.

As an example, here are the twelve lines of the Classic Reading attributed to Batman:

Batman Cold Reading

At times you are extroverted, affable, sociable, while at other times you are introverted, wary, and reserved. *Like many superheroes, Batman has two distinct personalities. This first Classic Reading line sums up Batman's dilemma perfectly.*

You have a strong need for other people to like you and for them to admire you. *Bruce Wayne, Batman's alter-ego, is concerned with how his superhero side is perceived by the public.*

Disciplined and controlled on the outside, you tend to be worrisome and insecure on the inside. *Batman most definitely projects control, but we know that Bruce Wayne agonises over his decisions.*

You have a tendency to be critical of yourself. *Batman is the most human of superheroes, and berates himself as much as any of us.*

You pride yourself on being an independent thinker and do not accept others opinions without satisfactory proof. *Batman is nothing more than a truth seeker, even in the face of adversity.*

You have found it unwise to be too frank in revealing yourself to others. *Batman's fear of revealing himself to others is pretty obvious.*

Your sexual adjustment has presented some problems for you. *Black leather outfits and Cat-woman come to mind. Tricky, no?*

While you have some personality weaknesses, you are generally able to compensate for them. *I think it's safe to say that both Batman, and Bruce Wayne, compensate for each other's weaknesses.*

At times you have serious doubts as to whether you have made the right decision or done the right thing. *Batman often wonders whether he should hang up his cloak and live the simple life of a civilian.*

You prefer a certain amount of change and variety and become dissatisfied when hemmed in by restrictions and limitations. *In Batman, Bruce Wayne transcends his human limitations. Change and variety are his day to day.*

Some of your aspirations tend to be pretty unrealistic. *Of all the things to aspire to, keeper of the peace and saviour of the world is rather far-fetched.*

You have a great deal of unused capacity which you have not turned to your advantage. *Even Batman can surprise himself as he digs deep to overcome his enemies.*

From Aragorn to Zorro, any protagonist can be fused with the Classic Reading. Using characters you love not only makes the process fun, it can help create connections that are almost impossible to forget. Make your own flash cards, one for each line, and juggle the order of the lines to find the best plot. You may be surprised how quickly you can learn the lines in tandem with your favourite characters.

10

The Imaginarium

Non-traditional oracles not only require a great deal of thought, it's a simple fact that many of their techniques, although fascinating, do not translate well into readings. Body language experts pore over hours of video footage, real interrogations can last days, and students of sociology often scrutinise extremely large data sets over many months. Conversely, readings last a finite time, are one to one, and are often performed in less than ideal environments. There is simply no way to replicate these scientific conditions in the context of a reading.

My favourite solution to this dilemma is to take Clients on a guided visualisation. This creates a shared experience, with enough Client feedback to give you something to actually read (or at least purport to read). Visualisations like this can be tailored to your oracle of choice, and the arbitrary, and not so arbitrary, thoughts of the Client can be interpreted accordingly.

Here's an example based loosely on the idea of interrogation:

> *'Hi Olivia, it's nice to meet you. I'd like you to close your eyes, and imagine you are sat at a desk in an empty room. I want you to tell me what you can see, feel and hear at all times. How are you sitting? What can you see? Is there anything else in the room. The door slowly opens. Who is at the door? The person enters, and sits opposite you. What do they look like, and what are they wearing? They push a piece of paper towards you, on which is scribbled a solitary word. What does it say?'*

Given this kind of questioning, Client feedback is almost impossible to predict. Let's take a look at some responses Olivia could have given:

- Olivia sat with her elbows on the desk on which was a mobile phone, some flowers, and a Vogue magazine

- She saw a map of Europe on the wall, and a small wall clock.

- Her father, dressed in formal attire, was at the door, and was in quite good spirits.

- The word on the paper was HOPE.

- During the visualisation, Olivia also mentioned the smell of perfume, being cold, and that she thought light was coming in from somewhere in an otherwise dark room.

If you're expecting me to interpret Olivia's responses, you're out of luck. She could have said literally anything, and the scope for interpretation is vast. You'll have to lean on the expertise you possess of the oracle in question, and to use as many JBCR riffs as it takes to make up for the deficit in your knowledge. You could do worse than pick up a cheap book on dream analysis for inspiration, and even Sigmund Freud's The Interpretation Of Dreams if you're feeling brave.

If you're charmed by the idea of a shared experience, see what happens should you treat the Client's feedback as a reading for yourself. Interpret your own flowers and magazine, and relay your own thoughts back to the Client. What do your own imaginary flowers look like? What is on the front cover of your own imaginary Vogue? The Client's responses put these thoughts in your head, so you may as well use them. Your own imagination, triggered by Client feedback, is a completely valid part of the reading process. Don't be afraid to see where both your imaginations take you.

A Waking Dream

You don't have to attribute your reading skills to any one oracle if you don't want to. Here is a longer, more generalised visualisation that can create a great deal of feedback.

'Close your eyes, and then put your hands over your eyes. Good. Now, I want you to imagine yourself floating alone in a bright empty space. It is beautiful, peaceful and calm, and you feel safe and happy. Although you have your eyes closed here, in the real world, I want you to imagine closing your eyes where you are now. Let me know when you have done that. That's great. Now, I want you to imagine yourself slowly descending. You get a sense that you are coming back to earth. You have no idea where you are, but as you descend I would like you to take a deep breath, and exhale slowly. Although your imaginary eyes are still closed, can you sense anything in your environment to indicate where you might be in the world?

As you descend further you can also hear sounds in the background, some close by, and some further away. What sounds can you hear close by? And what sounds can you hear in the distance? Do you recognise any of the sounds? How do they make you feel?

Finally, as your descent slows, you feel your legs shift to a sitting position before arriving comfortably on earth. Before you open your imaginary eyes, how does it feel? Can you sense what you are sitting on from touch alone?

Now, keeping your eyes closed in the real world, I'd like you to open your imaginary eyes and describe the scene before you. Are you inside, or outside? Is it daytime, or night? Can you see people, or animals? Does it resemble a place you know well?

You look to the right, and see is a table close by. Can you describe what's on it?

> *You look to the left, and see a wall full of photographs. Which one catches your eye?*
>
> *In the distance, you can hear a piece of music playing. What is it? How does it make you feel?*
>
> *That's great. OK, I'd like you to close your imaginary eyes one last time. Let the scene before you fads away. I'd like you to take one last deep breath before you drop your hands to your side, and open your real eyes once more. Thank you.'*

When creating scripts like this, it's important to avoid putting thoughts in the mind of the Client. It's also important to ensure they feel safe and happy at all times. Scripts such as this can generate a lot of feedback, and your analysis will be taken seriously, so I suggest trying your own scripts out on yourself. Record them, listen to them, and visualise them personally before trying them out on a Client. When you can't think of what to say, you'll always have the magic feather of James Bond Cold Reading to fall back on.

11

JBCR Conclusion

I hope you find the concepts found in James Bond Cold Reading to be of practical use. There's much food for thought in these pages, but I'd prefer you talked rather than procrastinated. Overthinking can be a huge problem when you're starting out so please, as always, Get Your Mouth In Gear. Pick a random JBCR line and start talking to a photo, stuffed animal or the steering wheel of your car should you have to. Pace the room at every opportunity, firing ideas and lines at imaginary people in make-believe scenarios. Get comfortable with your working environment, and treat your initial readings like dress-rehearsals. Audience management is key, but unless you say something there'll be no audience, nor reaction, to manage. Speak up!

Julian Moore
Stackpole, Wales 2023

COLD READING
GAMES

What Are Cold Reading Games?

- Do you find introducing yourself to strangers impossibly difficult?

- Are you worried you will run out of things to say on a first date?

- Would you like to inject a little more fun into your social life?

If you answered yes to any of these questions, this book could be for you.

Cold Reading Games will teach you enough about Palmistry, Graphology and Numerology to get you into trouble–the good kind. With an emphasis on getting your mouth in gear, Cold Reading Games delivers the tools you need to kick-start conversation, break the ice at parties, and banish awkward silences forever.

Let the games begin!

1
INTRODUCTION

Whether we're on a first date, or chatting casually with a potential friend or partner, most of us have lost our mojo at some point. When the conversation stutters to a halt, it can often leave us wondering what to say. Even the most outgoing of people can run out of steam occasionally, and for the introverted among us, there can be little steam to start with. Getting things going in these situations can be tricky, and keeping them moving can be even harder. And with complete strangers, many of us lack the courage to strike up a conversation at all.

Palmistry, Graphology and Numerology can help reduce Introduction Anxiety by focusing on other people's hopes and dreams. Rather than agonising over the perfect opener, readings help us leave our egos at the door, giving us the chance to converse with others in a meaningful way. With the pressure off to be anything but ourselves, there's a chance we will come across as interesting, by simply being interested in other people.

Although this book's sole intention is to get you talking, Cold Reading Games sources the classic interpretations for each oracle. So, should a more knowledgeable hobbyist question your methods, you'll have nothing to hide. I hope it gives you the confidence to make new friends, and to cultivate and enjoy the company of others you have yet to meet.

> **This book uses the same nomenclature found in James Bond Cold Reading, including the terms Reader, Client, oracle, truism, and trait. You can read more about these concepts in the Overview section page 15.**

How To Use This Book

Although you may have bought this book with an idea of focusing on one specific oracle, I encourage you to work through each section in order. The structure given in the Palmistry section is a great template for a reading of any kind. Many of its central concepts apply to both Graphology and Numerology, so I encourage you to read it first.

Yours And Mine

Throughout this book, I will be inviting you to compare your own readings with mine. Whether it's Palmistry, Graphology or Numerology, it's a useful exercise to compare your readings with those of others. To understand how it feels to be the focus of a reading, you need to at least attempt a reading for yourself. Comparing readings helps breed empathy, and the more you can learn about yourself, the more you can empathise with others.

Recaps

This book is about learning new things, with a focus on repetition and recall. There are recaps and exercises at spaced intervals, and answering them is a key part of getting things to stick. It may be hard work, but breaking the material into manageable chunks is far better than reading pages of forgettable text. It's fine to jump between chapters at first, but to learn things quickly it's best to work through each chapter in order. Focus on exercises you find difficult, and keep notes on those things that need more work.

Get Your Mouth In Gear

Apart from the recaps and exercises, you will also need to practice speaking out loud. Mouths have a way of mashing the greatest of thoughts to mincemeat, so you must verbalise your ideas at every opportunity. Throughout this book are exercises that encourage you to **Get Your Mouth In Gear**. Do not skip these exercises. Effective communication requires a voice, and it's essential you develop the habit of connecting your brain to your mouth. The apprehension new readers feel stems from a lack of experience rather than knowledge, and you'll feel less spooked once you've practiced delivering your words to an imaginary audience. Like an actor preparing for an audition, you will sound rough initially. You cannot correct that which you do not hear, and you need to get over the shock of hearing your own voice. Only then can you can work on finding a style and pace of delivery that feels natural. Don't be too hard on yourself, and do not be afraid to experiment with various tones, speeds, and approaches. There's no correct way to deliver a reading, but deliver you must.

To make things less abstract, each Get Your Mouth In Gear exercise uses an imaginary Client's name. Names conjure up a host of stereotypical images and ideas, so take advantage of this phenomenon and tailor your words to each Client accordingly. What does your Adrian look like? What do you think Belinda is wearing? Do Craig and Daniella make a good couple? They may not exist, but your brain can hardly tell the difference. Your memories of giving readings to these imaginary people cannot help but bring you confidence in the real world.

A Quick Note About Cold Reading

Broadly speaking, cold reading attempts to address the science behind readings, and is a measured look at the psychology in play during a reading.

Shut-eyes (psychics convinced of their ability) argue that cold reading practitioners lack psychic abilities. Psychologists argue that cold reading (a series of psychological ploys) goes some way to explain psychic ability.

Whatever you believe, this book will teach you to give readings with both eyes wide open, in ways that make sense, by using your own common sense.

Three Skills

Cold Reading Games teaches how to use Palmistry, Graphology and Numerology to help break the ice in social situations. The skills taught in this book are a means to an end, and **not** an excuse to become a Graphology bore. Readings may have their uses, but one must resist leaning on them too heavily should the conversation take its own course.

Here are a few of the many ways Palmistry, Graphology and Numerology can help strike up conversation:

Palmistry

Everyone has a palm, and even the most skeptical of people enjoy having their palm read. Nothing is required apart from a hand, and your eyes to see it. Remember that the head and the heart lines are common knowledge, and you will often meet people well acquainted with the lines of the hand. A Palmistry reading can be quite a tactile experience, so remember that one person's romantic is another person's creepy. The only downside to reading a person's palm (and there are almost no downsides) is that one palm reading can easily lead to another.

Women tend to be more receptive to Palmistry than men.

Graphology

Graphology (also known as Handwriting Analysis) requires a handwriting sample. This can be an excellent opportunity to learn a person's name, but requires a suitable environment, a writing implement, and something to write on. Graphology readings work well with larger groups as it's easy to explain, and people enjoy comparing each other's handwriting.

Men tend to be more receptive to Graphology than Palmistry.

Numerology

Numerology also requires a writing implement but, with a sprinkle of Graphology, we can establish a person's name, their mobile number and date of birth. Having these details at hand can take the sting out of requesting this information later, especially people you connect with. However, it's important to seek permission before getting in touch with someone you do not know well.

Westerners can be sceptical of Numerology, but those in the East take it more seriously.

Once you give readings, you will discover that one oracle leads easily to another, and a little knowledge can go a long way. The urge to over-deliver can be strong. It's best to spread your knowledge wide, and try to avoid any introverted tendencies you may have to hide in the safety of a lengthy reading. Keep readings open (and loud enough) to fuel the interest of others around you, and deliver just enough information to keep everyone coming back for more.

Conversation is a two-way street. You need to leave long gaps between statements and encourage Clients to help interpret what you see. Whether your focus is on a palm or a handwriting sample, people feel empathy towards those who take an interest. When the Client starts talking, you should not only listen, but give them the chance to pause and continue. You need to avoid interrupting and allow the Client to find their own pace. Getting to know another person is a gift, so do not squander the opportunity by making it all about yourself.

The Formula

As you work through Cold Reading Games and acquire some real-world experience, keep in mind this simple formula:

1. Tell the Client what you can see (the facts according to the oracle)
2. Offer your interpretation of the facts
3. Await a reaction
4. Interpret the reaction
5. Repeat

There's a lot more to giving readings than this simple five-step example, but I hope it dispels the myth that anything mysterious is going on during a reading. Readings are a process, pure and simple.

 **James Bond Cold Reading** features an exhaustive treatise on the mechanics of giving readings in Chapter 7, page 79.

TOP TIP: Readings are more like yoga than juggling, so resist the temptation to perform. Create a space for you and the Client, and inhabit it together. Take the pressure off yourself and, rather than attempting to deliver life-changing readings, enjoy any conversation you may create for its own sake.

2

BACKSTORY

Rather than admitting you learnt Palmistry, Graphology or Numerology from this book, it's best to fabricate a backstory. As well as being one less thing to worry about when asked, this imaginary justification for your skills can help develop your persona. A good backstory adds a personal twist to your readings, so don't hesitate to refer back to it where beneficial.

PALMISTRY BACKSTORIES

- 'I rented a villa just outside Rome with some friends a few years back, and there was a Palmistry book on the shelves. It's probably all nonsense, and our Italian was virtually non-existent. But it kept us entertained all week.'

- 'There was an old guy on the beach in Goa giving palm readings for a few coins. I looked some of it up when I got back home to see if he'd just made it up. It's all quite interesting, really.'

- 'My grandma used to read tea leaves, and she had an old bookcase with lots of strange and interesting books in it. I used to flick through some of them as a kid, and the Palmistry one stuck out as it had the most pictures.'

Although these examples are fictitious, there is a ring of truth about each of them. I have vacationed in European villas, I've been to Goa, and my late grandmother did, in fact, read tea leaves.

GRAPHOLOGY BACKSTORIES

As most people perceive Graphology as a forensic discipline, a convincing backstory is relatively easy to concoct. Graphology sounds like a useful skill to have and is a buzzword used in recruitment and crime novels. So how do you know so much about Graphology?

- 'I was sitting next to a guy on a plane once who was a forensics expert. He got me to write my signature down on a napkin and told me a few things about myself. His observations were pretty accurate and I've been kind of interested ever since.'

- 'I had a friend who inherited a box of signed photos and autographs from her grandmother. We used to look through them together, and compare their different handwriting styles. She got really into it, but I still dabble.'

- 'I saw a detective show where the team used a handwritten note to narrow down a pool of suspects. I googled Graphology while I was watching and my interest grew from there. If nothing else, I can spot a killer.'

There's not a shred of truth to any of these backstories. I have been on planes, looked at some autographs and watched TV, but that's about it.

NUMEROLOGY BACKSTORIES

It's hard to find someone who has not at least dabbled in Numerology. Many people wonder if the numbers in their date of birth mean anything, and kids often swap letters for numbers to create secret codes. The concept of numbers having their own intrinsic meaning is common, and many western buildings have no unlucky 13th floor. In China they often skip the 4th floor, as the number four signifies death.

- 'I've often noticed recurring patterns in my life, and the number 36 was not only my house number at school, but the street number of two houses I've lived in. I've always found numbers intriguing, and I'm fascinated by how they mean different things to different people.'

- 'I used to share a flat with a Chinese guy, and his mum was always giving us advice about what numbers to look out for in our lives. She used to draw numerology charts on the backs of restaurant napkins, and it kind of rubbed off on me. The numbers, of course, not the napkins.'

- 'My nephew studies pure maths at college and we got into a debate about the philosophy of numbers. I bought him a numerology book as a Christmas joke, but we ended up making number charts for the whole family. I can still remember some of it.'

The number 36 has always been a recurring number for me but, although I did once have a Chinese flatmate, I never met his mother. My nephew once asked an AI for their birth date, but arbitrary numbers cause little excitement for those with a background in pure mathematics.

Use these ideas as a springboard, but please ensure there is a hint of personal truth to your own backstories. When the source of your knowledge is called into question, you will feel a lot more comfortable with a half truth than a flat-out fabrication.

What's Your Excuse?

Before you go any further, create your own backstory for each oracle. Try to come up with as many quirky ideas as you can, including things that reflect your own experiences and interests. Don't be afraid to stretch the truth to make yourself look good, and be sure to have fun. You need to create backstories that are memorable, rather than boring and obvious, so jot a few ideas down and see which of them jump from the page.

- I know a few things about Palmistry because…
- I learned a bit about Graphology when I was in…
- I picked up some knowledge about Numerology when…

A Client may never learn the true source of your knowledge, but a vibrant, colourful and unique backstory can help set the scene for a reading. Make your backstories as interesting as possible, and don't be afraid to refer back to them as the reading unfolds.

3
PALMISTRY

Palmistry is often associated with crystal balls and gypsy caravans, but few people expect an old-fashioned fortune telling. This doesn't stop Clients being interested in any hidden strengths or talents they possess, nor uneager to discover how best to embrace their current hopes and fears. A reading can give a Client a different perspective on their life and, rather than telling a Client's fortune, a character reading can inspire them to discover it themselves.

No matter how short the reading, or how noisy the environment, your words will be taken seriously. Keep your moral compass in check, and look out for signs that you are in too deep. Should you feel uncomfortable with the direction a reading is taking, bring proceedings to a swift close, and feign ignorance if you must. No one requested an expert, and you certainly should not be promoting yourself as such. Keep things light.

Before we learn about the lines of the hand, it's important to consider the most appropriate mindset for both Reader and Client during a reading.

Talking And Listening

A Client will most likely say very little at the start of a reading, and expect you to do all the talking. Asking leading questions such as 'Does that make sense?' and 'Do you agree?' can help fan the flames of conversation and encourage a two-way dialogue. At first, these prompts will provoke short answers from the Client, and this is a time to pause and observe their reactions. No one likes an awkward silence, and you should always allow the Client to fill the gaps. At worst, these moments will allow you extra time to think.

Talk to the Client rather than their hand and, where possible, engage in face-to-face conversation. Don't make the mistake of focusing exclusively on their hand or, you'll miss their important facial cues. A Client may not say a lot at first, but at least you'll have their expressions to go on!

The Reading Bubble

You should always make the Client your sole focus, no matter what is going on around you. You can still include friends in the Reading Bubble, but the Client should never feel your focus drift. Many people love to be the focus of attention, and almost everyone likes to think they are special, so be sure to highlight any interesting traits on their hand. Be positive, upbeat, and lighthearted. Make people feel interesting, important, and unique. Give Clients your undivided attention, and do anything you can to make them feel special.

Rejection

When people see you giving a Palmistry reading, the chances are they will want one too. Giving readings can be exhausting, and you'll need to practice saying no, although be aware that some people can take this as an insult. Soften the blow by explaining how, in your depleted state, you could not possibly do their hand justice.

If someone you are interested in requests a reading whilst you are busy with another, a surefire way to see them again is to promise a later reading. Potential Clients never forget these promises, and will track you down later, often with friends in tow. Be sure to deliver on these specific promises if you can, but do not be afraid to keep these readings short if you're feeling burnt out. Smile, have fun and be courteous; everyone loves good manners.

> **TOP TIP:** Don't be afraid to let people know you are just starting out with Palmistry. Admitting you are a beginner puts the onus on others to help you become a better reader, and most people are happy to help when approached in this way.

P1 Lines Of The Hand

The three lines of the hand are the starting point for any Palmistry reading. Each line is judged by its CURVE and its LENGTH, giving us a couple of things we can say about each line during a reading.

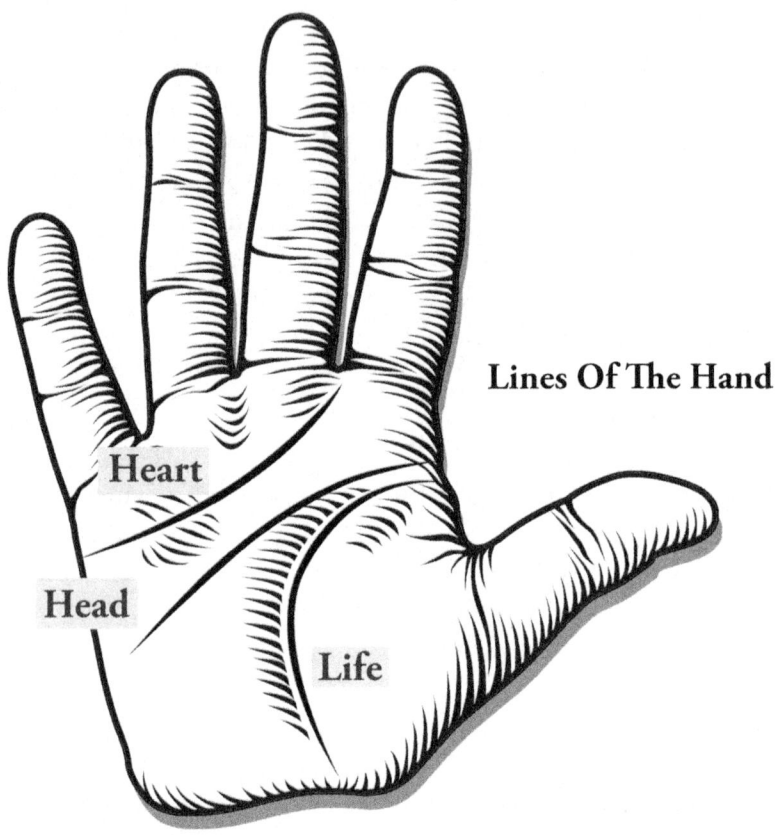

Lines Of The Hand

- The Heart Line is the top line nearest the fingers and represents the EMOTIONS
- The Head Line is the middle line and represents the THOUGHT PROCESS
- The Life Line is the lower line around the thumb and represents VITALITY or life energy

> **TOP TIP:** Prevent yourself getting the heart and head line mixed up by remembering that the (he) ART of piano playing involves the fingers.

Curve And Length

Analysis of the Heart Line and Head Line is very similar regarding their curve and length. We need only ask ourselves two questions when looking at the Heart line or Head line on a Client's palm:

- Does the line CURVE?
- What's its LENGTH?

If you can learn to attribute the name of each line to the answer to each of these questions, you'll be well on the way to using Palmistry to start a conversation.

For instance:

Heart Line

Does the heart line curve outwards (towards the fingers)?
- YES: Their heart is open
- NO: Their heart is closed

Is the heart line long?
- YES: Their heart is big
- NO: Their heart is small

Head Line

Does the head line curve inwards (towards the body)?
- YES: They think inwardly
- NO: They think outwardly

Is the head line long?
- YES: They think long
- NO: They think short

This may sound simplistic, but it really is the crux of the matter. Let us take a closer look at this idea.

Curved Lines

The CURVE of a line influences its meaning. Curves lend both lines either an outer or an inner characteristic.

- A HEART line that CURVES UP towards the fingers indicates someone emotionally expressive
- A HEAD line that CURVES DOWN towards the body indicates someone who internalises their thoughts

Straight Lines

When the lines are straight, these characteristics are diminished.

- A HEART line that is STRAIGHT indicates someone who ISN'T emotionally expressive
- A HEAD line that is STRAIGHT indicates someone who DOESN'T internalise their thoughts

Long Lines

The LENGTH of a line indicates how much of its trait a Client has. A person may have a lot of heart, but a short head line indicates quickness of thought rather than lack of thought altogether.

- A HEART line that is LONG indicates someone who is emotionally open
- A HEAD line that is LONG indicates someone who is a deep thinker

Short Lines

When the lines are shorter, their characteristics are also diminished.

- A HEART line that is SHORT indicates someone who ISN'T emotionally open
- A HEAD line that is SHORT indicates someone who ISN'T a deep thinker

These extreme distinctions can help make each line remarkably easy to remember, but people's lines can be difficult to judge in the real world. Don't be surprised if the words longish and shortish enter your vocabulary more often than not, and be prepared to use each line as a sliding scale of characteristics rather than a binary outcome. Judging people's lines can be rather tricky, but you will soon learn that ambiguity creates more interesting conversations than absolutes.

> **TOP TIP:** Sliding scale is definitely the key phrase here. Taking the full width of the hand to be 100%, and attributing a percentage to a line, such as 70% for a longer line or 30% for a shortish line, can help judge its power.

Comparisons - The Crux Of Any Reading

Line meanings are often contradictory, but rather than being a hindrance, you will discover their differences can give us a lot to say. You can get a lot of mileage from the head and the heart line, so share your limited but newfound knowledge at every opportunity. You need no more to strike up a conversation, and learning too much too soon can be a real problem. Only the experience of giving readings can make you a better reader and a head full of possibilities has a tendency to short-circuit the ability to speak, so start before there is a chance to overthink things. Learn a little at a time and put twice as much effort into talking about Palmistry than reading about it.

Saying that, you've got to know something, so we will now take each line individually. These are the standard meanings of the lines on the hand, and will meet the expectations of those who already know a thing or two about Palmistry.

> **TOP TIP:** If you're struggling to see the lines on a hand, try relaxing the hand by cupping it slightly. This makes the lines far easier to see, and can help you judge the lines accordingly.

Yours And Mine

Your Hand

It is can be useful (and a lot of fun) to compare your hand with that of the Client, so it's worth getting to know the lines of your own hand. Notice how it feels to agree or disagree with what you hand says about you, and imagine how this feels for a Client. When you find a trait too vague, attempt to clarify it and take special note of any lines you disagree with. Should you have a question about a line, answer yourself as if talking to a Client. As always, it's best if you do this out loud, and in your own words.

Once you've studied one of your hands, compare it with the other, and notice any differences and similarities there might be. It's normal to read a person's dominant hand (the one they use the most), but the less dominant hand is thought to represent the unconscious, well worth remembering when you're stuck for words, or wish to extend a reading.

My Hand

Here's a description of the lines of my own hand. How do your lines compare to mine?

- My heart line ends under my forefinger, and curves slightly upwards towards the fingers.

- My head line slants down, and stops about three quarters of the way across my hand.

- My life line sweeps down and around to the centre of my hand, where it splits into two.

We will refer back to my own hand as we work through each of the lines in turn.

HEART LINE
EMOTIONS

EXPRESSIVE VS SENSITIVE & OPEN VS CLOSED EMOTIONS

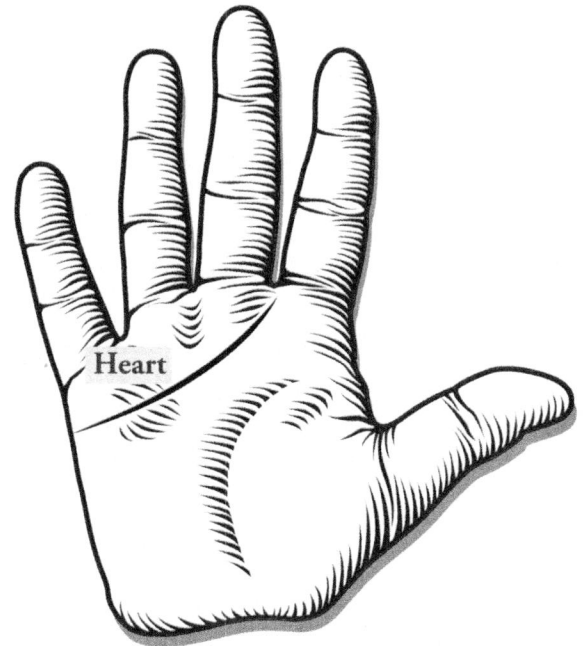

The heart line is the top line of the hand nearest the fingers and is all about EMOTIONS. We are interested in its CURVE and END-POINT. These two factors give us the base reading for the HEART LINE.

Does the heart line run in a straight line across the hand, or does it bend upwards towards the fingers?

- Heart line bends towards fingers = Open hearted / Expressive
- Heart line runs straight across palm = Less expressive / More sensitive and needy

> **TOP TIP:** We use our fingers to reach out and touch the world. A heart line that turns up towards the fingers shows a need to communicate emotions–an open book. A heart line that goes straight across the hand suggests a less emotionally communicative person–a closed book.

Where does the heart line end?

A long heart line shows an emotionally open individual, a short heart line shows an emotionally closed loner.

- Heart line ends beneath 1st finger (LONG LINE) = Emotionally open / Romantically idealistic
- Heart line ends beneath 2nd finger (SHORT LINE) = Emotionally closed / Loner
- Somewhere in-between 1st and 2nd finger (AVERAGE LINE) = Emotionally balanced

> **TOP TIP:** The first finger is used for pointing at what we want. A heart line that ends near the first finger indicates an emotionally decisive person. A shorter heart line shows a more emotionally withdrawn person.

Contradictions - Curve vs Length

You may find contradictions in one line alone. For instance, a short heart line that bends towards the fingers is contradictory, with its open-hearted and expressive bend signifying the exact opposite of its short, emotionally closed length. Most of us are well aware of how our better traits overcome those that are less useful to us, and highlighting contradictions like this can nudge the Client into opening up. This example could describe a person who appears confident on the surface, yet who closes down emotionally where more intimacy is required. Were the heart line long rather than short, its traits would be complimentary, and therefore not as interesting to talk about.

The art of giving a palm reading is to think out loud, whilst encouraging a response from the Client regarding the similarities, and contradictions, you may see. Rather than formulating your next great insight before you say anything, you need to verbalise your train of thought. To your own ears, it may sound amateurish and feeble, but to the person whose hand you are reading it will be nothing less than acutely interesting. The only mistake you can really make as a reader is to remain silent, so get into the habit of verbalising everything that comes to mind. Saying anything is better than nothing.

If you can think of something to say when you've only got one line to work with, you'll have plenty to discuss when you compare the characteristics of all three lines. We'll cover this in slightly more depth when we talk about Fault Lines.

In a Nutshell

A long heart line that bends up towards the fingers indicates an emotionally open and romantic person

which is the opposite of

A short heart line that runs straight across the hand indicates an emotionally closed and withdrawn person

Heart Line Recap

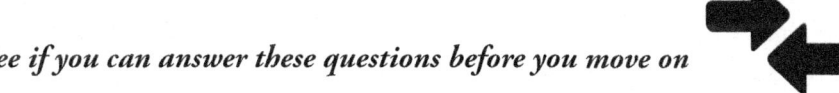

See if you can answer these questions before you move on

Get Your Facts Straight

These questions are to test your recall before moving on to the GYMIG section of this recap.

1. There are three main lines on the hand. Where is the heart line positioned?

2. What could a long heart line signify?

3. What about a heart line that ends beneath the second finger?

4. A Client's heart line runs straight across their palm. What could it mean?

5. What could a short heart line indicate?

6. What is the significance of a heart line that curves up towards the fingers?

Get Your Mouth In Gear

Explain to each of these Clients what their palms say about them. Speak out loud, and in your own words.

7. Derek's heart line is quite short, yet it curves towards his fingers.

8. Elizabeth's heart line is quite long and straight.

9. Ian's heart line is short and straight.

10. Georgina has a long heart line that curves almost right up to her fingers.

You may have committed the heart line meanings to memory, but the real work is in using this information to fuel conversation. On your first read through of this section, you may struggle with verbalising the last four questions, but with practice, you will soon get up to speed.

Once you've answered the GYMIG section above for the first time, try them a second time, and see how long you can talk for. Aim for ten seconds on this second attempt, and try to increase the time you talk by a further ten seconds during each subsequent effort.

Yours And Mine - Heart Line

Your Hand

Look at the palm of your dominant hand and analyse its heart line. Does it bend towards the fingers or run straight across the palm? Does it stretch completely over to the forefinger, your third finger, or somewhere in-between? Compare the heart line of your dominant hand with that of your non-dominant hand. If your dominant and non-dominant hands belonged to two different people, how would you say their emotional outlook differed?

My Hand

Now compare your heart line to mine. My heart line ends under my forefinger, and curves slightly upwards towards the fingers.

- Is your heart line similar, or radically different, to mine?

- If you were giving ME a reading, what could you say about my heart line?

- With only our heart lines to go on, do you think we would get along?

> **TOP TIP:** The longer a line, the more of that trait someone possesses. For instance, a long heart line indicates high emotions, a shorter one indicates a colder person. A long life line indicates lots of energy, a short one someone who is lacking energy. Slightly different is the head line–a long line indicates a detailed thinker, whereas a shorter one indicates a quick thinker. Take a moment to think about just how easy that is to remember.

STOP RIGHT NOW!

**You now know more than most people will
ever know about Palmistry.**

You know that a heart line that curves towards the fingers indicates an open-hearted and expressive individual, and that its length signifies emotions. It's more than likely, should you have been paying attention, you know a bit about the head line too. The fact is, you now know enough about Palmistry to start a conversation, so you should try to get talking at the nearest opportunity.

Imagine, for a moment, you knew nothing about Palmistry and you overheard someone talking about the lines of the hand. I think you'd agree that, in this situation, it's hard to resist peeking at your own hand for comparison. If your sneaky glance was noticed, it would not take too much to be drawn into some kind of exchange.

Now let's imagine you're the one doing the talking, showing people what you've learnt about the heart line in your local bar. It's obvious that your knowledge is limited, but some strangers at a nearby table have taken an interest and you ask them for a second opinion. Before long, everyone is looking at their palms, and someone adds that the life line is the one that wraps around the thumb. Another says they thought the head line is the middle line and before long, everyone's comparing hands. The ice has been broken, everyone's having a good time, no one is claiming to be an expert, and the conversation is flowing.

You don't need to be the star of the show, nor act as if you know everything about Palmistry to get people talking. No matter how much you learn, be mindful to play down your knowledge so you can engage in conversation rather than providing endless readings. Use what little you know as a tool for getting to know other people, and for them to get to know you.

You can read more about how to get things going in The Approach section of this chapter.

HEAD LINE CREATIVE VS LOGICAL & QUICK THOUGHT PROCESS VS DETAILED THINKING

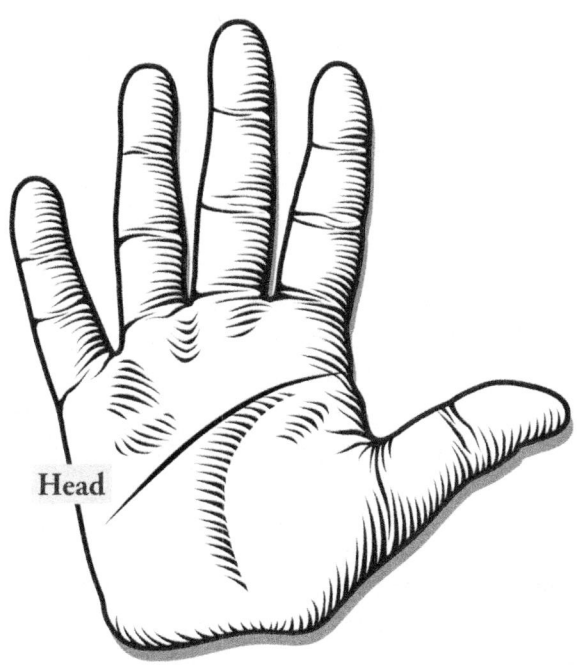

Head

The head line runs across the middle of the hand and represents the THOUGHT PROCESS. We are interested in its CURVE across the palm, and its LENGTH and PROXIMITY to the other hand lines.

Does the head line run in a straight line across the hand, or does it curve down towards the wrist?

In a similar way to the heart line, the curve of the head line is important. If the head line runs straight across the palm keeping towards the finger side of the hand, the thought process is drawn towards practicalities. If the head line curves away from the fingers somewhat towards the wrist, the thought process is reflected inwards towards the more creative inner self.

- Head line curves to wrist = Creative
- Head line is straight across palm = Logical / Down to earth

> **TOP TIP:** If a head line curves inward towards the body, the person is more inwardly creative, whereas a head line that is more towards the fingers is more practical and down to earth.

How long is the head line?

The longer the head line, the longer the person takes to think things through, whereas shorter head lines denote quicker thinking.

- Long = Detailed thinker
- Short = Quick thinker

> **TOP TIP:** People with long heads are known as eggheads, well known for an intellectual and scientific approach to life.

In A Nutshell

A short straight head line indicates a fast thinking practical person

which is the opposite of

A long curved head line indicates a thoughtful, creative person

Head / Heart Line Extra

How close are the head line and the heart line?

A heart and head line that touch indicates an impulsive Client whose romantic and practical sides can become intertwined. Separate lines indicate a Client able to keep their romantic and practical lives apart.

- Head line touches heart line = Impulsive
- Head line separate from heart line = Cautious

> **TOP TIP:** Mentioning head and heart line proximity is an easy way to get people to compare hands.

Head Line Recap

See if you can answer these questions before you move on

The first six questions are simply about getting your facts straight. The last four questions are about talking the talk, so attempt to answer them OUT LOUD as if you were talking to a Client.

Get Your Facts Straight

These questions are to test your recall before moving on to the GYMIG section of this recap.

1. Where is the head line positioned on the hand?

2. What could a long head line signify?

3. A Client's head line curves towards their wrist. What could it mean?

4. What significance could there be in a short head line?

5. What does a head line that intertwines with a heart line indicate?

6. What about when the head and heart lines are completely separate?

Get Your Mouth In Gear

Explain to each of these Clients what their palms say about them. Speak out loud, and in your own words.

7. Robert has a short head line.

8. Juliette has a head line that runs straight across their hand.

9. Frank has a very long head line that curves down towards his wrist.

10. Gabrielle has a short head line, yet it curves down towards her wrist. You also notice it touches her heart line.

YOURS AND MINE – HEAD LINE

Your Hand

Look at the palm of your dominant hand and analyse its head line. Does it bend towards the wrist or run straight across the palm? Would you say that your head line is long, or short? Compare the head line of your dominant hand with that of your non-dominant hand. If your dominant and non-dominant hands belonged to two different people, how would you say their thought process differed?

My Hand

Now compare your head line to mine. My head line ends at the start of my little finger, and is fairly straight as it runs across my palm.

- Is your head line similar, or radically different, to mine?

- If you were giving ME a reading, what could you say about my head line?

- With only our head lines to go on, do you think we would get along?

LIFE LINE
VITALITY

ENERGY & OUTLOOK

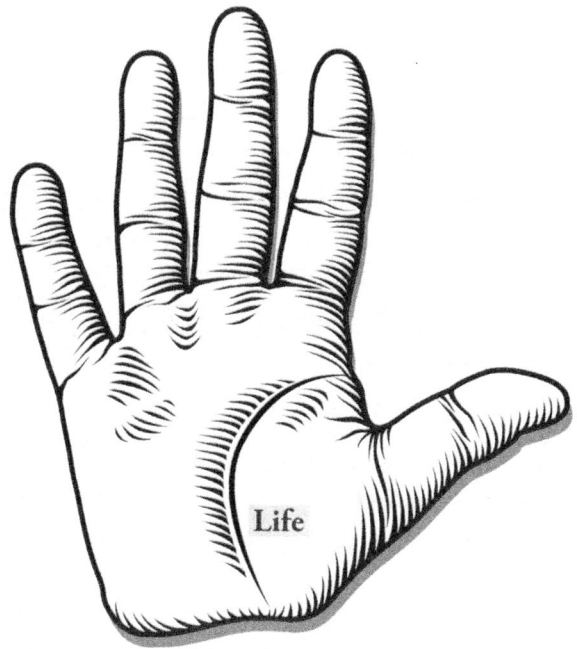

The heart line curves around the base of the thumb and represents LIFE FORCE. We are interested in its CURVE around the thumb and its LENGTH and START POINT.

How long is the life line?

People with long life lines that follow a large arc around the thumb have a lot of vitality and energy, whereas people with small life lines that hug the thumb can be quite lethargic.

- Long life line = More Energy
- Short life line = Less energy

> **TOP TIP:** Compare the arc the life line takes with the overall size of the hand to judge its length.

Where does the life line start?

Similar to the heart line, a life line that starts closer to the fingers indicates a more outgoing personality, whereas a heart line closer to the thumb indicates a more humble person.

- Life line starts near first finger = Ambitious
- Life line starts near thumb = Humble
- Life line equidistant between first finger and thumb = Practical

In A Nutshell

A long life line that starts near the fingers indicates an energetic, ambitious individual

which is the opposite of

A short life line that starts near the thumb indicates a less energetic, humble individual

Life Line Recap

See if you can answer these questions before you move on

The first five questions are simply about getting your facts straight. The last five questions are about talking the talk, so attempt to answer them OUT LOUD as if you were talking to a Client.

Get Your Facts Straight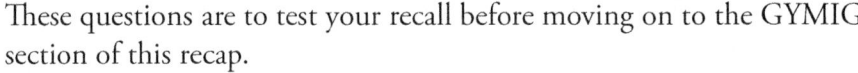

These questions are to test your recall before moving on to the GYMIG section of this recap.

1. Where is the life line positioned on the hand?

2. If someone has a short life line, what does it mean?

3. What does it mean if someone has a life line that starts quite far from their fingers?

4. What does a long life line signify?

5. If someone's life line starts near the fingers, what does it mean?

Get Your Mouth In Gear

Explain to each of these Clients what their palms say about them. Speak out loud, and in your own words.

6. Andrew has a long life line that starts somewhere between their first finger and thumb.

7. Simone has a short life line that starts near her fingers.

8. Xavier has a medium length life line that starts a fair distance away from the fingers.

9. Winona has a long life line that starts close to the fingers.

10. Guy's life line starts between his first finger and thumb, and is of average length.

It's possible you may have found it tricky to verbalise questions 8 and 10, as both hands are fairly nondescript. Something you're going to have to get used to is that, in the real world, the lines on people's hands are far less clear cut or obvious. You'll often struggle to judge whether a line is long, short, curved or straight. Therefore, it's important to practice Getting Your Mouth In Gear by talking out loud and practicing on real people. Luckily, the whole point of this book is to come up with excuses to socialise, so what better excuse than to admit that you're a Palmistry novice and need the practice!

Yours And Mine - Life Line

Your Hand

Look at the life line of your dominant hand. Would you say you have a long or short life line? Does your life line start nearer your forefinger, your thumb, or somewhere in between? Compare the life line of your dominant hand with that of your non-dominant hand. If your dominant and non-dominant hands belonged to two different people, how would you say their energy and outlook differed?

My Hand

Now compare your life line to mine. My life line starts pretty much exactly between my forefinger and thumb, and follows quite a long arc around the base of my thumb.

- Is your life line similar, or radically different, to mine?

- If you were giving ME a reading, what could you say about my life line?

- With only our life lines to go on, do you think we would get along?

P2 Bringing The Lines Together

Comparing the three lines of the hand makes up the bulk of most readings. Each line gives us two traits to work with, giving us the possibility of six traits across three lines. Talking through each line's traits is a just a warm up for the main body of the reading where, with as much help as we can rally from the Client, we compare and contrast the traits of all three lines together.

Seams Of Gold

The Japanese practice of Kintsugi involves fixing the cracks in ceramic bowls with lacquer and gold. Rather than being seen as scars, these imperfections give each piece a unique and interesting character. Similarly, a Client's contradictory traits can tell us more about their character than their complimentary traits, so rather than being afraid of the cracks in a Client's character, we should view them as Seams Of Gold, ripe for exploration and discussion.

For instance, a hand whose traits lean towards open, romantic and well balanced makes for a rather boring reading, but a hand with the more contrasting traits of loner, detailed thinker and ambitious would give both you, and the Client, far more to discuss. Seams Of Gold invite the Client to reconcile different aspects of their personality so, as a reader, you should learn to use the friction of opposing traits to your advantage.

Any interpretation you may give is up for discussion, and the Client should be allowed to digest what has been said through a series of pauses as you think out loud. Comparing traits like this can help invoke a sense of curiosity in the Client's mind, encourage dialogue, and work towards building a colourful and insightful reading.

> **TOP TIP: Although it's important to leave gaps in the conversation, holding a stranger's hand in silence for too long can feel creepy. Be chatty, not creepy.**

The Complimentary Hand
Here's an example of a hand whose traits are mostly complimentary

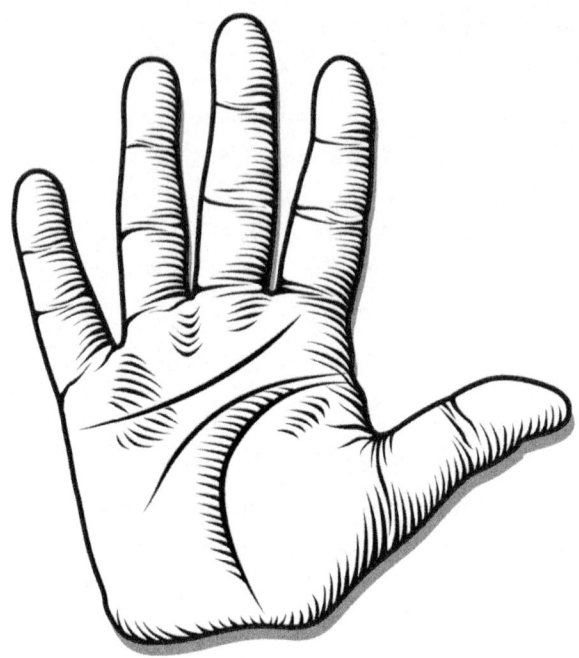

Heart Line
- Curved heart line = emotionally open
- Long heart line = romantic

Head Line
- Long head line = detailed thinker
- Curved head line = creative

Life Line
- Long life line = energetic

This hand's traits suggest an emotionally open, creative romantic and a practical, detailed thinker but, although this sounds nice on paper, it sounds pretty two-dimensional delivered as written. A string of bland yet positive statements make for a flat and characterless reading, and if there's one thing you need in a character reading, it's some actual character.

With a little work, we can eke out some discrepancies from these complimentary traits to make things a lot more interesting. If you can learn to give an interesting reading from a hand awash with similar traits, you'll find giving readings for more complex and contradictory hands an absolute breeze. However, no hand is truly dull, and the aim is to give engaging Palmistry readings to anyone, regardless of their hand's complexities or lack thereof.

Complimentary Hand Reading

Here's a recap of this complimentary hand's traits, followed by an example reading with its Seams Of Gold in **bold**. We'll get to the underlined and *italicised* sections in a moment.

- Emotionally open
- Romantic
- Creative
- Detailed thinker
- Energetic

'This is your heart line. <u>People with short heart lines tend to be quite closed but you have a long heart line</u> that reaches right over here to your first finger, showing that *you're quite open hearted. The heart line also curves towards your fingers, which can make you a little romantically idealistic.* So this could mean that you appear to be an open book to some people as you're quite outgoing, yet can be rather picky when it comes to partners.

'You have a nice long head line that sweeps down here towards your wrist, and this is definitely the line of a creative person, as people whose head lines curve towards themselves tend to be somewhat inward in their creative thoughts.

'That's interesting isn't it, **you've got this inward creative streak from your life line, yet as we saw in your heart line you're outgoing and open. Perhaps sometimes you find it hard to strike a balance between your outgoing side and your quieter, creative side?**

'You've got this long life line so you're not lacking in energy for whatever you want to do, and as it starts here kind of between the thumb and first finger you're quite practical when you want to be, and not always lost in a creative haze.

'Does any of that make sense to you?'

Seams Of Gold (in bold)

- **you've got this inward creative streak...you're outgoing and open… you find it hard to strike a balance between your outgoing side and your quieter creative side**

The Client's inner creative streak vs their outgoing and open trait give us a chance to put forward the idea that they struggle to reconcile the creative, and outgoing, sides of their personality.

Extreme Explanations (underlined)

- <u>People with short heart lines tend to be quite closed but you have a long heart line</u>

Explaining an extreme meaning of a line reinforces your knowledge, gets the Client involved, and gives you time to think. Emphasising a line's negative aspect can also add tension and drama to proceedings before revealing, thank goodness, that the line on a Client's hand does in fact point towards its more positive and upbeat opposite.

In-Line Contradictions (italicised)

- *you're quite open hearted...a little romantically idealistic... you appear to be an open book to some people... yet can be be rather picky when it comes to partners*

From the heart line alone, we can pull the idea of open-hearted vs romantically idealistic. This vague clash is ripe for interpretation and goes to show that almost anything can be contradictory should you frame it correctly. There is no positive without a negative, and even James Bond's positive qualities got him into plenty of trouble.

The Curse And The Cure

We all like to think that our strengths overcome our weaknesses so, whenever you find a negative trait, an opposing yet redemptive trait can help balance things out. None of us are perfect, but the ability to overcome our imperfections is a large part of what makes us who we are. Explaining to a Client how they overcome one trait with another can be hugely empowering, whilst taking the sting out of having to say something less than stellar.

Examples:

> *'You have an abundance of this, which more than makes up for that'*
>
> *'So that means you tend to be a bit quiet and introverted, but you more than make up for it with a huge amount of inner determination, shown by this'*

False Traits

Some of the greatest conflicts arise when a Client flat-out disagrees with what their hand says about them, and who are we to disagree? Only a Client knows what they are truly like, and you should encourage them to help flag false traits. These hand-vs-person clashes are part and parcel of any reading, and should be treated with curiosity rather than panic. A seemingly unfair trait can jolt even the most placid of Clients to speak up for themselves, and putting things straight can be a great catalyst for further conversation. For that reason alone, it is almost always a good idea to find at least one false trait during a reading, no matter how small.

False traits don't always have to provoke the Client, however. Should you sense a trait may be false, you can incorporate it into your reading by playing a negative trait off a Client's perceived positivity and conviction. It is the same technique as The Curse And The Cure, but pits a Client's hand trait against your perception of their actual character.

For instance:

> *'This line tells me that things haven't always been that easy for you. You've had to do everything you can to become the person you are today but, as a confident and assured person, you've had a fair amount of success.'*

You don't have to start with a negative hand trait. Sometimes it works better to talk about (what you deem to be) a Client's personality, before discussing a negative trait.

For instance:

> *'I can see you're a confident and assured person with a fair amount of success, but this line tells me things haven't always been that easy. You've had to do everything you can to become the person you are today.'*

It should be noted that a pep-talk may not go down at all well for a Client whose life has comprised a series of hardships. Rather than being overly optimistic and upbeat with these Clients, one must keep things more down to earth. Acknowledgement of their difficulties is often all they need to hear.

> **TOP TIP:** We all struggle with conflicting thoughts and ideas about who we are, and what we should do with our lives. Some Clients are almost entirely defined by their insecurities, and highlighting their positive traits may be challenging. It's not your place to disrupt the psyche of the more pessimistic among us, so be wary of being overly positive in these cases. The cure needs to match the persona of the patient, and some people do not want to be cured.

 Lenses can be of great use when giving any kind of reading. You can learn more about them in Chapter 7 of JBCR, starting on page 79.

P3 Finger Meanings

Many people know at least something about the lines of the hand, but few know that the fingers themselves possess any significant meaning. However, like each line on the palm, the fingers have specific traits that can be interpreted in a variety of ways. Finger meanings are not only novel but fun to read, and can be a great starting point for a conversation.

Each finger represents a particular trait and, somewhat like the lines of the palm, we'll be looking at their length and size, and whether they curve or bend towards each other. We can use the easy to remember acronym **ARCC** to remember their meanings of **A**mbition, **R**esponsibility, **C**reativity and **C**ommunication and, as the fingers of the hand naturally create an arc when you hold them out, it could not be easier to remember!

Let's take a moment to familiarise ourselves with the basic meaning of each finger.

1st Finger - AMBITION

We use our index finger to point at what we want and where we want to go. It's no wonder this finger signifies AMBITION.

2nd Finger - RESPONSIBILITY

For some people, the second finger's sole purpose is to make a vulgar gesture, but we all have the choice to be rude or keep calm. This flippant sign of the bird can help remind us we must all take responsibility for our actions.

3rd Finger - CREATIVITY

Few people use their third finger to any great extent, but musicians use their third finger regularly. For most people, the third finger signifies a source of untapped creative potential.

4th Finger - <u>C</u>OMMUNICATION

The relevance of this finger to communication remains a mystery, but its meaning is easy to remember. Using the internationally recognised gesture for 'call me', create an imaginary telephone by putting your thumb to your ear, and speaking into your pinky.

INTERPRETING THE FINGERS

The length of a Client's fingers is relative, and all four should be viewed together, at least initially, to best decide whether any one finger is dominant. To help judge the length of each finger, it's often useful to straighten the palm and push the fingers lightly together. The larger a finger, the more its traits have dominance over the others, so a longer than average second finger would suggest a responsible type who gets by using common sense. Conversely, a noticeably shorter second finger would suggest irresponsibility and rash decision making. Should the length of the fingers appear pretty average, you can try taking their overall size into account. You may find some Clients with one finger thicker than the rest.

Another important thing to look out for is the bends in a Client's fingers. To help judge the bend in each finger, it's useful to seek gaps between fingers when both straightened and at rest. A bend in a finger weakens its trait slightly, and weak fingers lean towards stronger fingers for support.

Here's an analogy that is not only useful as a memory aid, but a concept that Clients love: **The Palm Tree Analogy**. Imagine the fingers are four palm trees in a line. The strongest trees stand completely straight while the others lean on them for shelter. For instance, an ambitious first finger leaning towards a straight and responsible second finger could indicate ambition somewhat subdued by a keen sense of responsibility. A third and fourth finger that lean towards each other could indicate a Client's ability to use both their creative and communicative skills in tandem.

Discussing the fingers in this way is ripe for interpretation, and can be compared and contrasted with the lines of the hand. Do the traits shown in a Client's finger match those found in the lines of their palm? Does a smaller than average communication finger completely contradict a long, strong and outwardly curving heart line?

> **TOP TIP:** You can add the idea of individual trees either having enough, or too little, water to thrive. By looking at the soft area of the palm beneath each finger (the mounts) you can see whether these mounts are raised, suggesting a surplus of water energy or dipped, suggesting a deficit.

You can get a lot of mileage out of The Palm Tree Analogy. Here's one of the ways you could use it to start a conversation:

> *"Did you know that each finger on the hand has its own meaning? The second finger is all about responsibility, whereas the third finger is about creativity. Fingers bend towards each other for strength, so do you think you're more responsible than creative, or the other way around?"*

IN A NUTSHELL

The meaning behind each finger can be remembered using ARCC

Some fingers are stronger than others

Fingers lean towards each other for support

Finger Meanings Recap

See if you can answer these questions before you move on

Get Your Facts Straight

1. Each finger has its own trait. What four letter acronym can we use to remember them?

2. What does the first finger represent?

3. What does the second finger signify?

4. Which finger is all about creativity?

5. Which finger is all about communication?

6. What does it mean when one finger bends towards another?

7. What could a completely straight finger signify?

8. What could you say about a finger that is comparatively larger than the others?

9. What could you say about a finger that is comparatively smaller than the others?

10. What could a particularly short finger signify?

Get Your Mouth In Gear

Explain to each of these Clients what their fingers say about them. Speak out loud, and in your own words.

11. Arnold has a surprisingly short little finger that bends towards his third finger.

12. Beth's second and fourth fingers both bend towards her third finger.

Her forefinger is straight.

13. Eric's fingers are mostly straight, although his second and third fingers do bend towards each other somewhat.

14. Francesca's second finger is straight and prominent. Her first finger leans towards it.

Yours And Mine - Fingers

Your Hand

Look at the fingers of your dominant hand, and take a moment to gauge their relative lengths. Do you think you have a dominant finger, or do they all appear relatively equal in size? Also notice how your fingers either bend towards, or away from, each other. Do any of your fingers bend towards another other for support, and is any finger straighter than the others?

Compare the fingers of your dominant and non-dominant hand. If your dominant and non-dominant hands belonged to two different people, how different would you say they were in their general outlook?

My Hand

Now compare your fingers to mine. My forefinger and second finger both bend towards my third finger, and my third finger bends towards my second finger. My little finger does not bend at all.

- Are your fingers similar, or radically different, to mine?

- If you were giving ME a reading, what could you say about my fingers?

- With only our fingers to go on, do you think we would get along?

P4 The Approach

This section is about drawing people into a conversation about Palmistry.

A technique that works well in the right circumstances is to 'notice' a potential Client's hand, and engage them in conversation about it. This may sound ridiculous (we all have hands, after all), but the idea is to get caught in the act of taking an interest. You don't want to stare blankly at people's hand like a lunatic, but you do need to look inquisitive and curious, a relatively natural behaviour for a student of Palmistry. With a bit of luck, you'll get a look rather than a punch, your excuse being that their hand is interesting or unique in some way. People don't meet palm readers every day of the week, so with some brief eye contact and a quick apology, you'll most likely be asked what you can see. As long as you are direct and upfront about their hand, you can disperse any notion you were ogling their purse, wallet, drink or significant other.

You'll soon learn that many people take great care of their hands. Some wear a ring, or a multitude of rings. Some have painted nails, some have false nails, and some have painted false nails! You often see hands with tattoos, hands with paint on or under the nail, hands that are discoloured from some kind of physical work, and hands that are beautiful. Complimenting someone on their hands is one of the safest compliments you can give, so don't be shy. It may be unusual, but unusual is good, and a compliment is a compliment.

If possible, use this technique on people accompanied by a friend or group of friends. This can help take the heat off the situation, and can increase the odds of a positive response from at least one person ('Hey, what about my hand?'), whilst avoiding any creepy-stalker vibe.

Example One

You're having an awkward moment at a bar with someone you hardly know. They're quiet, nervous, and somewhat aloof. Your friends have disappeared, and you'd like to get to know this person better. You decide to take an interest in their hands, to the point where you get a reaction.

Them: (looking up a few times to see what you're looking at) *'Are you looking at my watch?'*

You: (smiling) *'No, at your hands! I'm looking at your fingers, they're really long.'*

Them: (somewhat taken aback) *'Oh, thanks!'* (awkward pause) *'So...'*

You: *'People with long fingers tend to be quite creative. I just wondered if you were an artist or something, or did something creative?'*

Them: *'Oh, what else can you tell?'* (offers you their hand)

This may seem far-fetched, but the idea is sound. If you start with a compliment, you can't go wrong.

| **TOP TIP: Don't be creepy #1**

Example Two

You are in a club. In amongst a group of friends is someone you'd like to start a conversation with, but they are distractedly tapping on their mobile phone. Their impressive false nails are on full display.

You: *'Your nails are cool, how long does it take to get those nails on every day?'*

Them: (lowering phone) *'Huh? Oh, I dunno, twenty minutes?'*

You: *'You've got really long fingers, those nails make them look even longer! People with long fingers are really creative you know. Are you an artist or something?'*

Them: (laughs) *'No! I work in a shop. Why? Are you some kind of guru?'*

You: (smiling) *'No, but can I take a look at your hand? I think *it might be interesting.'*

Them: (putting phone away) *'Sure, go ahead!'* (offers you their hand)

Nails like this can take a long time to get right, so any show of appreciation is likely welcome. If someone looks like they want to be noticed, don't be afraid to compliment them on the effort they have made.

It's easy to tell whether someone is doom-scrolling, rather than actively texting a friend, and people mainly tap away at their phones through sheer boredom. None of us intend to waste a night out by staring at our screens, but it happens with alarming regularity. You can use this to your advantage!

I hope these examples encourage you to try this technique out for yourself. Of course, you'll need to discover what works for you, but if you trust your instincts, you'll be amazed what you can come up with on the spur of the moment.

> **TOP TIP:** Secretly examine as many hands as you can in public and notice the multitude of ways people adorn their fingers. With a bit of luck, you'll be caught out and forced to give a reading on the spot!

You're So Creative

Everyone likes to think they are creative. Telling someone they're creative stands a good chance of being true, and if they do turn out to be an artist or musician, you're golden. The other great thing about creativity is that even the least creative people in the world believe they possess some kind of creative potential, hidden deep and untapped in their bones. Creativity seems to be something we all want, and people are happy to apply it liberally to any aspect of their personality they see fit.

The bottom line is, whatever you say about a Client's hand to get their attention, say something about creativity.

'I like the way you've painted your nails. It's really creative.'

'You have really soft looking hands. Are you an artist or something?'

'I like your ring. Did you make it yourself? Your hand looks very creative.'

> **TOP TIP:** Take a moment to consider how a Client's hand choices (nails, rings etc) might affect a reading.

THE REAL WORLD

You need to face up to the fact that there is never a perfect time or place to give readings. Lines can be hard to read, people are not always that forthcoming, and it's hard to hear what people are saying in loud environments. It's easy to lose your flow when interrupted, and you cannot always hold people's attention as much as you'd like. This is the harsh reality, and no amount of knowledge can prepare you for the experiences you may encounter giving readings. To ensure that your readings are bullet-proof further down the line, you need to practice giving real-world readings as soon as you can. Only the experience of giving readings can make you a better reader.

However, you've got to start somewhere, so consider the following points before you attempt your first palm reading.

QUESTIONS QUESTIONS

You may give character readings, but some Clients will ask you questions about their future. The bulk of these questions will concern current, and possibly future, relationships. Do not offer advice about the future. Turn the conversation towards the Client's character to help them determine whether they are doing the right thing, or heading in the right direction. Use your common sense and agree with how people feel about their romantic choices, rather than advising what to do about them. Let Clients answer their own questions by breaking things down into simpler questions regarding their feelings and morals. By all means, play devil's advocate to show how certain situations could pan out, but do not at any point take any side of a romantic argument, or tell people what to do.

> **TOP TIP: Don't give advice, ever. Let people answer their own questions.**

Availability

Within certain age-ranges, relationship-based questions often reveal a Client's romantic status. Most times, you will know pretty quickly whether someone has a partner. While you're giving a reading, you'll often hear people say 'That's just like my girlfriend' or 'That's what my boyfriend is always saying' not just because it's true, but because the Client wants you to know they are romantically unavailable. It could also be because they are looking to point you in their direction of their single friends. Whatever the reason, this is all useful information and can help your reading enormously.

You should also take your own age into account, as the dynamic of a reading can shift depending on whether you are younger, or older, than the Client.

> **TOP TIP: Don't be creepy #2**

Best Friends

No matter how long you spend giving a reading, Clients are usually left wanting to know more about themselves. This can make it hard not to end readings on a slight downer. A good way to stop this happening, whilst drawing more attention to yourself, is to bring the subject around to best friends.

Clients love to see what their best friend's hands reveal about them so they can compare notes. It's amazing how people open up when there's a close friend to join in with, and if you give a reading to one person in a group, their friends will look on with great interest. Those traits a Client disagrees with are often greeted with a chorus of approval and laughter from their friends, so take advantage of these situations, and have some fun.

Partners

It's one thing to answer a Client's compatibility questions, but giving their partner a reading is another thing entirely. It can be fun, but only if they're willing and receptive. Not all partners are up for it, and declining the push to give a Client's awkward partner a reading could be doing them a favour.

If a Client's partner seems responsive and you decide to give them a reading, try making them look good. Keep things light-hearted, and see if there's anything genuinely amusing you can say regarding their attitude towards their other half. You'll have already spent some time learning about the original Client, so it's easy to find commonalities between their hand and that of their partner. Don't be afraid to seek contradictions either, as these can inject some humour into proceedings. Banter is to be encouraged.

If a partner is not keen on having their palm read, you can always turn to Graphology. Men tend to find Graphology more interesting than Palmistry, and you will learn how both this and Numerology can be useful in different situations later in this book.

> **TOP TIP: If the partner of the Client or their friends turn negative for any reason, it's time to leave.**

Palmistry On A Date

Whether it's your first or second date, chances are your potential partner is interested in you. Conversation can still run dry on these occasions, so there is no harm in bringing up the subject of Palmistry. Comparing hands can be quite a tactile experience, and encourages all kinds of interesting questions regarding compatibility. It's also a great way to get to know each other better. Your date will probably want to know as much about your hand as theirs, so it is best to be prepared. You have all the time in the world to make your own palm reading interesting and amusing, so spend the time on it and you will never be caught out.

As you are the one with the knowledge, you can describe your hands as one hundred percent compatible should you wish, but don't be afraid to highlight their differences. No two people are perfectly alike, and you do not want to appear too eager. If you can make fun of yourself and admit your less attractive qualities, while taking the occasional friendly dig at your date, you will get along just fine. Just don't take it all too seriously.

Examples

'My heart line is a fair bit longer than yours, which means I've been known to cry watching soppy films while you'd prefer to watch Terminator 2.'

'Your head line shows that you're a bit of a worrier, and have a tendency to overthink things. My head line is really short, which means I'll never understand why you overthink things.'

'Your palm is very soft. Feel mine, it's rugged and tough. However, this line shows I'm useless at putting up a shelf.'

'You have long fingers like mine, which suggests we're both creative and you're probably even more sentimental than me. We'd probably argue a lot about our favourite TV shows, and what music to listen to.'

> **TOP TIP:** Be aware than particularly attractive Clients can often get fed up with being stared at. Focusing on their hand can help them, and you, feel a lot more comfortable.

P5 Bringing It All Together

Let's bring the lines of the hand together with what we've learnt about the fingers, and see how they can be combined to make a cohesive reading.

Palmistry Reading Example

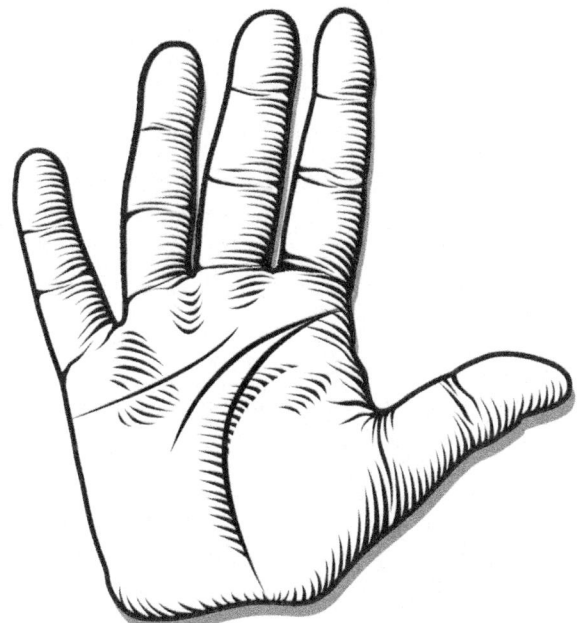

This is a hand with a short straight heart line. The head line is short and curves towards the wrist. The life line is long and starts somewhere close to the first finger. The first finger is strong, and two of the other fingers bend towards it.

The Lines

- Short straight heart line = Less expressive / Sensitive and needy / Emotionally closed / Loner
- Short curved head line = Creative, quick thinker
- Long life line near first finger = Energetic and ambitious

The Fingers (The Palm Tree Analogy)

- 1st Finger long, strong, straight = Ambitious
- 2nd Finger bends towards 1st finger = Responsibility leaning on ambition
- 3rd Finger bends towards 2nd finger = Creativity leaning on responsibility
- 4th Finger normal and straight = Communication not a problem

Although going over the lines of the hand before tackling the fingers can help give your readings a sense of structure, a cold list of traits can help us spot complimentary and contradictory traits. If we put them into one long list, it gets even easier.

- Less expressive / Sensitive and needy / Emotionally closed / Loner
- Impulsive
- Creative, quick thinker
- Energetic and ambitious
- Ambitious (again)
- Responsibility leaning towards ambition
- Creativity leaning towards responsibility
- Communication not a problem

Combining the lines with the meanings of the fingers gives us a huge amount of information. If you were to recite these meanings to a Client, the reading would be static and boring. To make things more interesting, we'll compare contrasting traits to fuel the conversation.

Before I give an example reading, let's look at the two conflicting sides of this hand's traits:

> **A:** There is a lot of ambition here, a short head line showing a creative, quick thinker, a long life line that starts near the first finger and a strong first finger that the other fingers bend towards.
>
> ***Summary: Ambition / Creative / Quick Thinking***

B: Somewhat contrary to that, we have a short heart line that runs straight across the palm showing a sensitive and needy person who is rather emotionally closed, and who appears to forsake responsibility in pursuing their dreams.

Summary: Sensitive / Needy / Emotionally closed

The Palm Reading

Here's an example reading I could give based on this hand. I'm starting completely cold and, as is always the case, I've had no chance to see the Client's hand in advance.

'So you have quite an interesting hand here, let's take a look. Do you know anything about Palmistry? Well, this is the heart line, and it runs here from the side of the hand across your palm underneath your fingers. I must admit, I've seen longer heart lines but don't worry, it doesn't mean you're heartless! It could mean that you're slightly more reserved than most people. I'm not sure if that makes much sense, so can we just look at the other lines to see what we can see? [PAUSE]

'It's funny, your head line is this one here, and although it's quite short too, did you know that a short head line actually means a quick thinker? Instead of taking forever thinking things through, there's a chance you can be quite impulsive at times. [PAUSE]

'Also you'll see the head line is bending down towards your wrist. Are you creative at all? [PAUSE]

'Ok, so you have a job that you hate, but I guess yes, you should get back on to writing that book you've started and s stopped a few times! There's definitely a creative streak here. And you know what? That could be what that short heart line is all about; you need time alone to do your thing. [PAUSE]

'So this is your life line but don't worry, I can't tell how long you're going to live. But you do have this big long curving life

line which shows you certainly have enough energy to throw into things once you put your mind to it. [PAUSE]

'Actually, that ties in quite nicely with the next thing, your fingers. Did you know that your fingers also tell a story too? Well they do, and in fact your forefinger here, your pointing finger, is quite strong, and all these other fingers seems to be bending towards it. Your pointing finger is all about getting what you want and knowing where to go in life, and I'd say that this finger is definitely the strongest one of the fingers on your hand. I take it you can be quite stubborn? [PAUSE]

'That's interesting, because although you know what you want and part of you isn't that scared of getting it, I do feel that perhaps that, if anything, it's the introverted streak I noticed in your heart line holding you back a bit. [PAUSE]

'So let's take a look at these other fingers. This one next to your index finger is all about responsibility, and like the next one along, the creativity finger, both of them are leaning somewhat towards your stronger pointing finger. In Palmistry, it's said that fingers that lean against others are relying on them for strength.[PAUSE]

'Yes that's right, your drive to succeed in whatever you do does come at a cost. I'm not saying you're irresponsible, or not creative as we've seen your creativity in your head line, but it could be that your single-mindedness can come at a price.

'If you look here at your little finger you'll see it really has nothing to do with the other fingers, it's out on a limb! The little finger is all about communication, a bit like if you pretend holding an imaginary telephone to your head and the finger is the mouthpiece. Yup, that's how I remember it too! Anyway, it seems you don't really have a problem with communication. [PAUSE]

'Yes, that does seem somewhat contradictory to this heart line of yours! I guess that's what makes you interesting, and what

makes you able to write books. Some of the time you really need to be on your own, but you also have this massive outgoing streak which enables you to get what you want.

'So people say there's two sides to every person, and I think that's reflected in your hand. What do you think? [PAUSE]

'Cool. Thanks for showing me your hand, to be honest I'm not really sure about this stuff but I'd like to hear more about that book of yours…'

A few notes on this example:

- Although the initial splash of a reading can feel overwhelming, it's best to dive straight in. The shock can actually help your nerves from getting the better of you.

- I describe what I can see and explain my findings as I go. This is for my benefit as much as the Client's, and gets me talking immediately.

- I pause often and await a reaction from the Client. Initially, a flicker of recognition will do, but the hope is to increase engagement as the reading unfolds.

- I do my best to avoid negativity, especially at the start of a reading. Starting off with a sensitive and needy short heart line would be rude, so I started with the heart line instead.

- I lean into the Client's feedback, as people interpret what you are saying against a backdrop of their current hopes and dreams. This Client is quick to indicate they are unhappy with their job, and interprets the suggestion of a creative streak as indicative of their literary ambitions.

- Just because a reading has wound down does not mean the conversation is over. The hope is that, by the end of a reading, I will have learnt enough about the Client to keep chatting should I wish.

Lines Of The Hand Nutshells

Here are the lines from each Palmistry nutshell. It's easier to remember the meanings of each line if we think of them as a point between two extremes, although in practice, you'll find the lines more vague than this.

HEART LINE - EMOTIONS
(top line, nearest to fingers)

A long heart line that bends up towards the fingers indicates an emotionally open and romantic person
which is the opposite of
A short heart line that runs straight across the hand indicates an emotionally closed and withdrawn person

HEAD LINE - THOUGHT PROCESS
(middle line)

A short straight head line indicates a fast thinking practical person
which is the opposite of
A long curved head line indicates a thoughtful, creative person

Life Line - VITALITY
(curves around the base of the thumb)

A long life line that starts near the fingers indicates an energetic, ambitious individual
which is the opposite of
A short life line that starts near the thumb indicates a less energetic humble individual

General Pointers

Lines towards fingers - more outgoing and outward / practical
Lines away from fingers - less outgoing and more inward / creative
Long line - more of a line's trait
Short line - less of a line's trait

Palmistry Recap And Quiz

There now follows a randomised collection of Palmistry questions culled from each recap. As before, we begin with the simple questions and end with the GYMIG questions, but I urge you to answer ALL the questions out loud for this recap, taking note of any you may struggle to verbalise. It's easy to get tongue-tied when you're starting out but, to make progress in the fastest time possible, you need to be brutally honest with yourself.

Remember these simple rules:

- The meaning of each line is summed up in its name

- The length of each line signifies how much or how little of its trait a Client possesses

- Curves towards fingers are outward and practical, curves towards the wrist are inward and creative

- ARCC can help you remember the finger meanings of Ambition, Responsibility, Creativity and Communication

- Use the Palm Tree Analogy to explain how the fingers interact with each other

THE BIG PALMISTRY QUIZ

Get Your Facts Straight

1. There are three main lines on the hand. Where is the head line positioned?

2. Where is the heart line positioned?

3. Where is the life line positioned?

4. If a Client has a long heart line, what does it mean?

5. What does it mean if a Client has a short head line?

6. What does a long life line signify?

7. How about a short heart line?

8. What does a long head line indicate?

9. How about a short life line?

10. What is the significance of a head line tangled with a heart line?

11. What significance is there in a life line that starts quite far from the fingers?

12. A Client's heart line goes straight across their palm. What could it mean?

13. What about if their head line curved towards their wrist?

14. What could completely separate head and heart lines indicate?

15. What could a life line that starts near the fingers indicate?

16. What about a heart line that curves up towards the fingers?

17. What does it mean if a Client has a heart line that ends beneath their second finger?

18. Each finger has its own trait. What four letter acronym can we use to remember them?

19. Which finger is all about communication?

20. What does the second finger signify?

21. Which finger is all about creativity?

22. What does the first finger represent?

23. What does it mean when one finger bends towards another?

24. What could a completely straight finger signify?

25. What could you say about a finger that is comparatively larger than the others?

26. What could you say about a finger that is comparatively smaller than the others?

Get Your Mouth In Gear

Explain to each of these Clients what their palms and fingers say about them. Speak out loud, and in your own words.

27. Michael has a long life line that starts somewhere between their first finger and thumb.

28. Sarah has a short life line that starts near her fingers.

29. Douglas has a medium length life line that starts a fair distance away from the fingers.

30. Janine has a long life line that starts close to the fingers.

31. Fred's life line starts between his first finger and thumb, and is of average length.

32. Maureen's heart line is quite short, yet curves towards their fingers.

33. Harold's heart line is quite long and straight.

34. Chelsea's heart line is short and straight.

35. Alberto has a long heart line that curves almost right up to their fingers.

36. Monique has a short head line.

37. Christopher's head line runs straight across their hand.

38. Yolanda has a very long head line that curves down towards her wrist.

39. Mikey has a short head line, yet it curves down towards his wrist. You also notice it is tangled with his heart line.

40. Michelle's third finger is large for the size of her hand, and both her second and fourth fingers bend towards it.

41. George's first finger is clearly dominant. His first and second fingers bend towards each other.

42. Brenda's fourth finger is quite small. Her second and third fingers lean towards each other.

43. Tom's fingers are all equally straight, although his first finger bends slightly towards his second.

44. Christine's fingers all bend towards her comparatively long and straight second finger.

If you can answer even a quarter of these questions you're good to go, so don't be afraid to try readings on friends, acquaintances and strangers as soon as you can. Sharing your knowledge will make you feel good, give you confidence, and reinforce what you've already learnt. You'll also start noticing Client reactions, and come to see readings as a shared experience. Don't overthink things, and don't present yourself as a Reader. Share what you've learnt so far on your Palmistry journey, and see where it takes both you and your Clients.

P6 Palmistry Reading Practice

Get Your Mouth In Gear #1

Highlight the various traits shown on the lines of these hand examples, as if explaining each trait to a Client. Speak out loud as you go, but do not worry too much about giving readings just yet. In each example, focus on as many individual traits as you can. Also, highlight any finger traits using the Palm Tree Analogy.

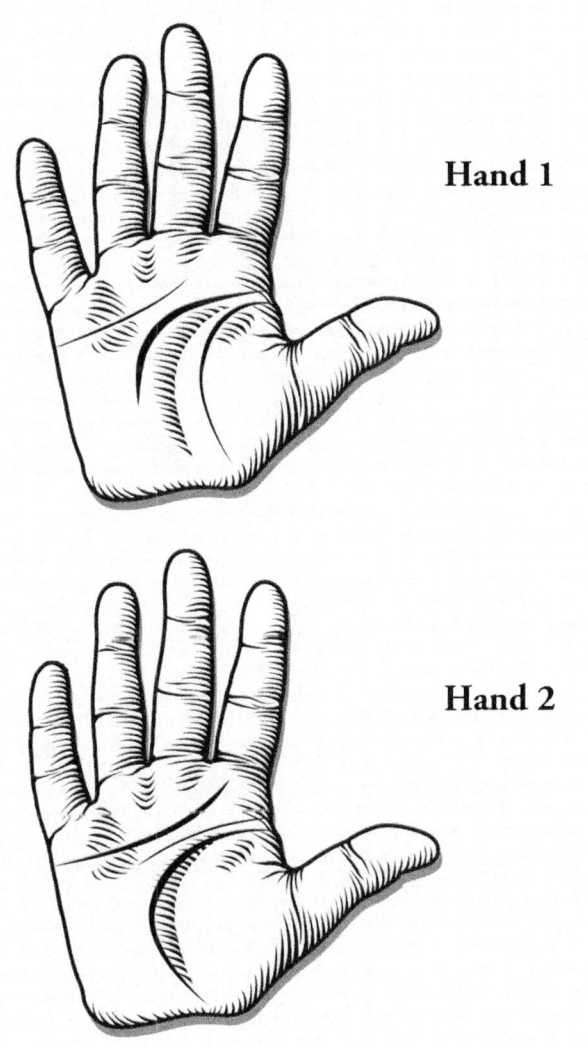

Hand 1

Hand 2

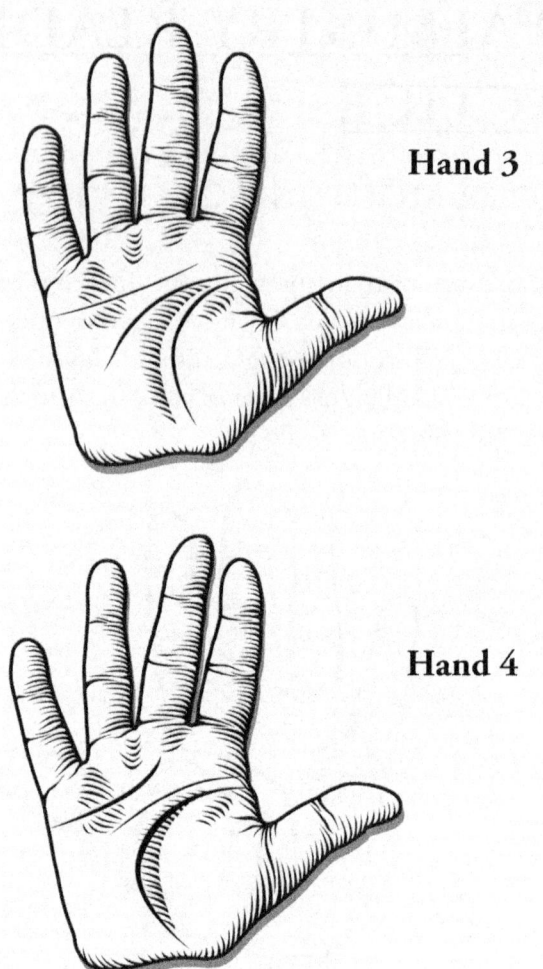

GET YOUR MOUTH IN GEAR #2

Give each of these Clients a reading based on the hand examples above, considering each Client's gender, age and background. Speak out loud as if they were in front of you, and try to talk for as long as you can.

5. Glenn, 59 years old. Architect, thick head of hair, designer glasses, nervous energy.

6. Daphne, 41 years old. Single mum of three, hair in a bob, sportswear, independent and active.

7. Charlie, 37 years old. TV executive, short hair, smart jacket, likes historical documentaries.

8. Phoebe, 19 years old. Apprentice chef, shaved head, retro jacket, dreams of her own restaurant.

Tackle the examples in order initially, matching each hand with each Client. Once you've done that, mix and match the hands with different Clients, and notice how much or how little each reading changes using different combinations.

P7 Palmistry Conclusion

Of all the oracles taught in this book, Palmistry is one of the few that can be performed on anyone at the drop of a hat and, for that reason alone, more pages have been devoted to this chapter than any other. This chapter not only covers the meanings of the lines and fingers, but also delves into some of the broader concepts behind giving readings. Consequently, this chapter can be used as a template for your oracle of choice, and the next two chapters focus more on basic mechanics than on reading technique. Come back to this chapter should you find your Graphology or Numerology readings lacking, and see whether its structure and ideas, especially those surrounding contradictions, can apply to your chosen oracle.

If you have enjoyed this Palmistry section and want to learn more, please consider my book '**Palmistry–Palm Readings In Your Own Words**' for a more in-depth discussion on palm readings. The book is accompanied by ten flash cards that can be downloaded from my site for free, and you may find these useful whether or not you have the book. They can be printed onto index cards, or stored on your phone or tablet to be viewed at your leisure.

Should you wish to take your palm readings to the next level, there is also a tick sheet available, cleverly entitled '**Palmistry Tick Sheet**'. Tick sheets serve both as a memory aid for you, the reader, and as a souvenir for Clients. You should check it out.

Best of luck–the future is in your hands!

4
GRAPHOLOGY

People can be quite receptive to Graphology. Few people have had their handwriting analysed, giving it a high novelty factor. One advantage Graphology has over Palmistry is the ease with which one can interpret several samples at the same time. The most important loops, curls and dots are easy to point out, and people love comparing each other's signatures. Once you've shown a group of people the things to look out for, they'll compare each other's scrawls almost immediately. If there's no pen or paper to hand, they're usually not that hard to obtain. There's often a pen lurking about somewhere, even if you need to borrow it from the friendly bar staff, and there's always a newspaper or napkin about.

Graphology can be used in much the same way as Palmistry to get a conversation going. You can also use Graphology in tandem with a Palmistry reading, or use it on its own for those moments when Palmistry feels inappropriate. Graphology can be far less intimidating than Palmistry because it is, literally, more hands off, with no pressure to tell people's fortunes. Clients will expect an insight into their character; nothing more, nothing less.

This Graphology system is designed to be memorable and fun, and if you have even half a handle on Palmistry, you'll find Graphology a breeze. As before, the meanings are taken from traditional Graphology, so you will not get caught out should you cross paths with a professional. The system revolves around the Client writing the word **typical** in lower case, followed by their signature.

To show how and why the word typical is useful, there now follows an example of how one could introduce idea of a Graphology reading to a Client.

The Typical Male / Female

> *'Do you see yourself as a typical male or female? Let's discover if what you think about yourself matches reality. If you write the word typical in lower case, plus your signature, I can help you uncover the truth.'*

Everyone likes to think they are unique, and this opening gambit is almost irresistible. The letters T, I, Y and P are some of the most revealing letters in Graphology, and the dot above the I is also interesting. Getting people to write the word typical alongside their signature also allows you to learn their name (if it's legible, that is).

This Graphology method comprises six easy to remember stages:

- Inspect the letters T and I of **typical**

- Inspect the loops (or lack of them) in the letters Y and P of **typical**

- Inspect the slant (whether the word leans backwards or forwards) of **typical**

- Inspect the baseline (whether the word rises or falls on the page) of **typical**

- Analyse the **signature** to assess its content and style

- Compare the Client's **typical** handwriting with their **signature**

> **TOP TIP:** Getting people to write the sentence 'I am a typical female' or 'I am a typical male', signed as a formal declaration can be a lot of fun.

G1 The Letters T & I - Graphology Golf

The first stage is to look at the letters T and I in tandem, using something I call Graphology Golf. Graphology Golf not only helps us remember the meanings of the letters T and I, but gives us a fun way to interpret them. Graphology Golf shows us how a Client approaches life, and whether their attitude either helps, or hinders, their life goals.

Remember, we are looking at these letters as they appear in the lower case, written word **typical**:

- The letter **T** represents the **golfer**
- The crossing of the **T** represents the **swing** taken at the **golf ball**
- The dot of the **I** represents the **golf ball**
- The **I** represents the **flag** / hole in the green being aimed for

The way someone swings at a golf ball tells us something about their attitude. Their accuracy in getting the ball above the flag can indicate how successful they are at achieving their goals.

- Did they aim ridiculously high and overshoot?
- Did a small but direct shot result in a hole in one?
- Does the ball land close to the flag against all odds?

Examples

What can we say about this person in our imaginary game of golf?

From this handwriting sample, we can see a high and hard swing has overshot the hole considerably. This is likely to be someone who has a great deal of enthusiasm but often over-stretches themselves.

This person has taken a perfectly measured and straight shot and landed right on the flag. This denotes a person who takes quick decisive action and focuses on detail.

This person has got the ball on the flag even though they have driven it into the fairway. Probably someone who neither looks too far ahead nor harbours wild ambition, but often gets what they want, regardless.

> **TOP TIP: Dyslexics think phonetically and may spell typical with an i instead of the y, such as 'tipical'. It's up to you how you deal with this, but it can be fun comparing the accuracy of two golf balls rather than one. Current ambition vs future ambition, perhaps?**

High Ball No Ball

The height of a Client's dot can vary. You will find some dots directly above the stem of the I, but at some distance (height) from the main letter. These are still considered perfectly accurate shots, albeit with a dose of lofty ambition. The higher the dot, the more idealistic the outlook. If there's no dot, we can assume the ball is missing in the rough. Clients who neglect to draw a dot may be unsure of where their goals lie, and may put energy into the wrong things, and lack a clear sense of purpose.

You can get a huge amount of mileage from Graphology Golf. It's great fun, easy to remember and Clients love it. If there's one thing you can bet Clients will try out on their friends once you are gone, it's Graphology Golf.

> **TOP TIP:** Some people will not have listened, and will either write the word typical with a capital T or entirely in capitals. If you are giving a reading to a group of friends, it can be amusing to single out 'the one who never listens'.

IN A NUTSHELL

Graphology Golf can show us how a Client approaches their goals and ambitions

The swing is the crossing of the T, the I is the flag and the dot of the I is the golf ball

YOURS AND MINE - GOLF ANALOGY

Your 'typical' Sample

Write the word **typical** in your normal handwriting. Try not to overthink it and make it as natural as possible—you need to write it so it reflects your day to day handwriting. Once you've done that, apply the Golf Analogy technique to the T and the I, and see if you agree with what the swing, ball and flag have to say about your personal approach to life.

My 'typical' Sample

Now look at the T and the I from my own sample below, and do the same thing. What can you glean about my approach to life using the Golf Analogy, and how does it differ, if at all, to your own?

typical

STOP RIGHT NOW!

You now know more than most people will ever know about Graphology.

A basic understanding of Graphology Golf is more than enough to keep people entertained. Once a Client has written the word typical, or any other word that includes the letters T and I, you can tell them about their general approach to life, and how it helps or hinders their ability to reach their goals.

You will find fewer opportunities for giving Graphology readings than Palmistry, so you will need to be a little more upfront to get things started. Graphology Golf provides an ample chance for friends to compare notes, so aim for groups rather than individuals, and learn to accommodate the crowd. There's safety in numbers, so be sure not to single anyone out should you want a warm reception, and be prepared to take advantage of situations that involve pen and paper.

You can read more about how to get things going in The Approach section of this chapter.

Golf Analogy Recap

See if you can answer these questions before you move on.

Get Your Facts Straight

1. What does the line that crosses the T signify?

2. What does the letter I signify?

3. The dot of the I is important. What does it represent?

4. In what way is the crossing of the T important?

5. How does the placement of the I dot reflect on a Client's character?

Get Your Mouth In Gear

Five Clients have written the word typical, and you are applying the Golf Analogy to each sample. See if you can think of something to say for each of them, based on the letters T and I. Speak out loud, and in your own words.

6. Nick's dot of the I seems completely missing.

7. The cross of Angela's T is tiny, but the dot of the I is perfectly placed, if somewhat high, above the I.

8. Jon's T has been crossed with a large stroke up and to the right, but the dot is placed just above the letter I.

9. Karen's crossing of the T is very short and pointing down, and the dot of the I is high and to the left.

10. Lance's T has a straight, but medium-sized T bar. The dot of the I is not only high, but far over to the right.

G2 The Letters Y and P - Sociability And Physicality

The letters Y and P can both have a curve or loop when written in lower case. The size of the loop in the letter Y indicates how sociable someone is. The size of the loop in the letter P indicates how physical someone is.

- **Y = YOU** - the larger the loop the more open the person.
- **P = PHYSICAL** - the larger the loop the more physical the person.

Some people draw large loops, some draw small loops and some people hardly draw loops at all, indicating a deficit of a trait. The idea is to look at the loops together, and to judge whether their traits complement each other or not.

Here are four examples of Y and P loops. See if you can say something about each one before reading their descriptions.

- Small Y / large P loop - Socially selective, could make up for it with physical activity
- Large Y / small P loop - Gregarious, may prefer to spend time socially rather than in physical activity
- Small Y / small P loop - Socially selective, not that physical, tends to be a loner
- Large Y / large P loop - Gregarious and physically active, probably enjoys team sports and social outings

These last two examples show the extremes. Loops that are tight with hardly any loop at all indicate a quieter type, whereas large, open loops in both letters indicate the more outgoing among us.

Comparing the size of the loops of the letters Y and P can give you a lot of mileage and, when combining this with Graphology Golf, you'll have a lot to compare. However, one should judge not only the loops against each other, but also against the size of a Client's overall writing style. If the loops are incomplete or end abruptly, this can indicate frustration socially and/or physically.

IN A NUTSHELL

The size of a Y or P loop indicates how much or little of a trait a Client possesses

Y - YOU loops show how much of themselves Clients project into the world

P - PHYSICAL loops show how physical people are

YOURS AND MINE - Y AND P

Your 'typical' Sample

Look at the Y and the P from your **typical** handwriting sample. Do the loops of the Y and the P agree with what you believe about yourself?

My 'typical' Sample

Now apply the same loop rules from the Y and the P to my **typical** sample (see page 176). What do these letters tell you about my openness and physicality, and how do they differ from your own?

> **TOP TIP:** If you are having a problem judging the loops or there are not any at all, try comparing the lengths of the stems instead.

Y and P Recap

See if you can answer these questions before you move on.

Get Your Facts Straight

1. What does a small Y loop signify?

2. What about a large P loop?

3. What would a large Y loop signify?

4. And a small P loop?

5. What could you say to a Client with a large Y and P loop?

6. If their P loop was smaller, how would that change things?

7. What could you say to a Client with a small Y and P loop?

8. If their P loop was larger, how would that change things?

Get Your Mouth In Gear

Four Clients have written the word typical. See if you can come up with something to say for each of them, based on the loops found in the letters Y and P. Speak out loud, and in your own words.

9. Angela's sample features a Large Y loop, and a small P loop.

10. Bernard's sample has a Large Y loop, and a large P loop.

11. Trina's sample contains a Small Y loop, and small P loop.

12. Tim's sample has a Small Y loop, and a large P loop.

G3 Slants And Baselines

Client's handwriting is rarely straight and tends to slant either forwards or backwards and, without lined paper to use as a baseline, it often fluctuates across the page. The meaning of these tendencies are fairly self-explanatory.

- The slant of a Client's handwriting indicates their slant on life. Do they lean into it, or away from it?
- The rise and fall of a Client's handwriting indicates their outlook. Are they upbeat or downbeat?

Slants

No Noticeable Slant - Normal

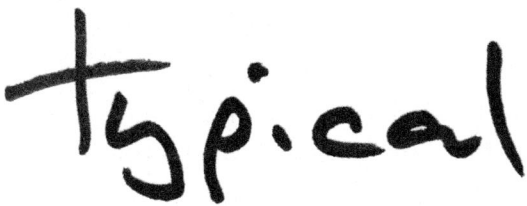

Most people's handwriting leans somewhere between being perfectly upright or leaning slightly forward.

Slanting Forward - Emotionally Responsive

Handwriting that slants forward to the right indicates an emotionally responsive person.

Slanting Backwards - Emotionally Withdrawn

Handwriting that slants backwards to the left indicates an emotionally withdrawn person.

Some Client's handwriting slants can be extreme, so be wary of describing them as overbearing or withdrawn if they are obviously nothing of the sort.

IN A NUTSHELL

Handwriting slants forward -
People that lean towards you find you interesting

which is the opposite of

Handwriting slants backward -
People that lean away from you are more guarded

TOP TIP: It is very rare that someone's handwriting slants both to the left AND to the right over the course of a sentence or phrase. However, if you see this rare occurrence, it is seen to represent someone with a dual personality.

TOP TIP: Lefties (those of us that are left-handed) have a very different writing style to those who are right handed, so judge the slant of a Client's handwriting accordingly.

Baselines

Writing that rises up the page indicates an upbeat attitude, whereas writing that falls down the page indicates a more downbeat outlook.

It's usually easy to spot whether a Client's handwriting rises or falls across the page. If you're finding it hard to judge, use the top and bottom edges of the paper as your baseline, and imagine how the handwriting would look with a straight line drawn beneath it. If the paper itself is the issue (such as a sheet ripped from a magazine) then judge its rise or fall in relation to the Client's signature if possible.

Straight baseline - Normal

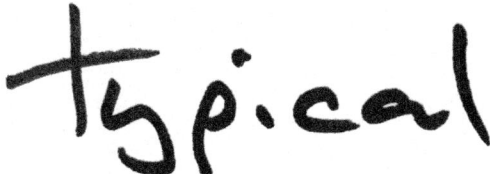

Most people's handwriting runs fairly straight across the page, but it is not unusual to see a small rise.

Rising baseline - Upbeat

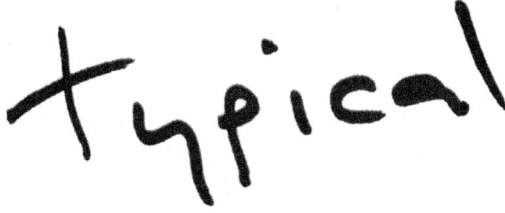

An extreme rise can indicate an extremely optimistic person.

Falling baseline - Downbeat

Falling baselines indicate a downbeat outlook.

Someone who has a wavy or uneven baseline could be rather up and down, as you can imagine!

In A Nutshell

**Handwriting rises up the page -
Client has an optimistic outlook**

**Handwriting falls down the page -
Client has a pessimistic outlook**

Yours And Mine - Slants & Baselines

Your Slants And Baselines

Take another look at your **typical** handwriting sample and take note of whether it slants and / or if it rises or falls on the page. If it slants, do you agree with what its slant says about you? And if its baseline is less than straight, do you agree with its meaning?

My Slants And Baselines

Refer back to my **typical** sample on page 176. Using the rule of slants and baselines, what could you tell me about my personality? How similar are my slants and baselines to your own and, based on our signatures alone, how do you think we would get along?

SLANTS AND BASELINES RECAP

See if you can answer these questions before you move on.

Get Your Facts Straight

1. What does it mean should a Client's handwriting leans backwards?

2. What does it mean should it lean forwards?

3. What if it leans neither backwards, nor forwards?

4. What does handwriting that rises up the page signify?

5. What if it slopes down the page?

6. What if a Client's handwriting runs straight across the page?

Get Your Mouth In Gear

Come up with something to say to each of these four Clients, using the slants and baselines found in their typical handwriting sample. Speak out loud, and in your own words.

7. David's handwriting slants forwards and rises up the page significantly.

8. Laura's handwriting slants backwards and runs straight across the page.

9. Eric's handwriting neither slants forwards nor backwards, and falls down across the page.

10. Harriet's handwriting slants backwards significantly and rises slightly up the page.

G4 Signature

The **signature** of a Client is their most personal scribble and, depending on its spelling, can be analysed it much the same as the word **typical**. If there is a T or an I in their signature, you can use aspects of Graphology Golf. If there is a Y or a P you can look at their loops, and you can also judge the signature's slants and baselines.

If there is a disparity between the way a Client writes the word typical and the style of their signature, you have the makings of an interesting analysis.

Names

A signature is a personal and conscious choice. We can decide which of our names to use, which to leave out, and which to make entirely illegible. The names the Client uses in their signature give us an insight into how they want to be perceived.

Full Name - Steadfast / Trustworthy

Julian Moore

Someone who writes their full name is usually a person who is steadfast and trustworthy.

Initialed First Name - Formal / Less Open

J. Moore

Someone who misses out their first name by using an initial is more formal and less open about themselves.

First Name Only - Open / Informal

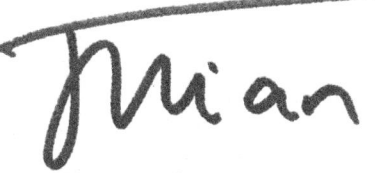

A signature that is simply someone's first name shows someone who is very open and informal, even flamboyant.

Surname Only - Serious

A surname only can show seriousness.

IN A NUTSHELL

A Client's signature should be viewed as a personal statement

The names a Client uses in their signature can indicate how formal, informal or serious they are

---

TOP TIP: As mentioned in the previous section, always remember the person is connected to their hand and signature; the way they write it, the way they use a pen, their entire attitude should be taken into consideration when judging their handwriting. You are not analysing people's handwriting by post or email, you are engaging with the person face to face on a personal level, so do not forget to use your common sense and natural intuition.

Style

Signatures have their own style, and some Client's signatures border on the artistic. Signatures are a form of expression, and can give us an insight into how people want to be seen by the outside world. Much of it comes down to common sense, but here are a few tips to get you started.

Can you read it?

A large, illegible signature made in a flurry indicates bravado, egotism and an outgoing personality. However, a smaller, equally illegible signature could be of someone who signs their signature a great deal, such as a doctor or a lawyer.

Is it underlined?

An underlined signature can indicate the need to project a sense of power and conviction.

Does it have a full stop?

A full stop at the end of a signature can show a need for assertion. People who write full stops at the end of their signatures can be quite stubborn, and like to get their own way.

In A Nutshell

The style of a signature can indicate how a Client would like to be seen by others

You can use common sense to interpret a signature's style

Yours And Mine - Signature

Your Signature

Write your day-to-day signature, the one you would use to sign a cheque or letter, and notice how much or little of your name you use, as well as its overall style. I think you will agree that your signature sums up your overall demeanour pretty well. It is, after all, your most personal of scrawls. If you dislike it, I suggest you change it!

My Signature

Here's my signature. What do you make of it, and how do you think the names I use and the style of my handwriting reflect my personality? Is your signature anything like mine, and if so, do you think we have anything in common?

Julian Moore

Signature Recap

See if you can answer these questions before you move on.

Get Your Facts Straight

1. What could you say about a Client who uses their full name in their signature?

2. What about a Client who wrote their surname, but only an initial for their first name?

3. How would you describe a Client who signs only their first name?

4. What about if they only used their last name?

5. What two things could an unreadable signature signify?

6. What could you say about someone who underlined their signature?

7. What does a full stop at the end of a signature signify?

Get Your Mouth In Gear

Come up with something to say to each of these five Clients out loud, and in your own words.

8. Steven uses his full name in his signature, and it is quite large and flamboyant in style.

9. Marie has underlined her signature, which comprises her surname only. There's little style to it.

10. John's signature is nothing more than a tiny squiggle.

11. Barbara's signature is a huge underlined squiggle.

12. Harry's signature is small, straight and neat, and uses both his first and second names.

G5 The Graphology Approach

This section is about drawing people into a conversation about Graphology.

Graphology is less abstract to laypeople than Palmistry, and the lines of the hand can seem arbitrary and obscure in comparison as we all write, we all have a signature, and it's easy to compare handwriting styles. Once a specific set of Graphology traits are explained (such as Graphology Golf) they are easily remembered, making it easy for those listening to get involved. Graphology's disadvantage over Palmistry is that, although most people carry their hands with them, the same cannot be said of a pen and paper. The Client also has to be sufficiently engaged to write what is required in the first place, so you cannot launch straight into a Graphology reading. It needs setting up first.

Fortunately, there's nothing strange about carrying a notebook and pen around, and there is usually something to write on nearby in the form of a receipt, beer mat or napkin. A scrap of newspaper will often suffice, and bar staff are happy to furnish you with a pen should you ask nicely. Even with the tools in place, however, striking up a conversation using Graphology can be tricky, and the chances of 'noticing' a potential Client's handwriting is near impossible unless you're way too close for comfort. Some situations lend themselves to Graphology more readily than others and, although remarking on a stranger's crossword can be a little strange, at least the tools needed for a reading are in play.

It may feel like a bit of a cheat, but one way to segue into a Graphology reading is to strike up a brief conversation about Palmistry first. Touching briefly on the head and the heart line is more than enough to transition into Graphology, the excuse being you'd like to see whether the lines and traits on the Client's hand match their signature. Should they be receptive to that idea, you can then request a **typical** handwriting sample and take things from there.

A bolder way to strike up a Graphology conversation is to request feedback on your personal, 'new-you' signature. The ruse is, by making a conscious decision to change ones signature, we can all project a more positive future for ourselves. Of course, asking strangers what they think of your new signature(s) is merely a conversation starter, but if you want to try this strategy, I suggest creating some new signatures well in advance. The results can be interesting and rewarding, and can help give you an insight into why people settle on their current signatures.

Example One

You're having an awkward moment at a bar with someone you hardly know. They are quiet, nervous, and somewhat aloof. Your friends have disappeared, and you'd like to get to know this person better. You decide to take an obvious interest in their hands, with an aim to talk way more about Graphology than Palmistry.

Them: (looking up a few times to see what you're looking at) *'Are you looking at my watch?'*

You: (smiling) *'No, at your hands! I'm looking at your fingers, they're really long.'*

Them: (somewhat taken aback) '*Oh, thanks!*' (awkward pause) '*So...*'

You: *'People with long fingers tend to be quite creative. I just wondered if you were an artist or something, or did something creative?'*

Them: *Oh, what else can you tell?'* (offers you their hand)

You: (looking at their hand) *'I'm not too knowledgeable, I only got into this recently. I'm more of a Graphologist. I can see that you're quite romantic as you have a long heart line.'*

Them: '*What's a Graphologist?*'

You: *'I'm interested in people's handwriting. You can learn a lot about people from their handwriting.'*

Them: *'Hang on a minute...'* (grabs a pen and paper from their bag)

You: (continuing) *'I can also see that your head line is short. Looks like you're a quick thinker. You got that pen of your bag pretty quick! If you could just write your signature, we can start with that.'*

This is almost identical to the first Palmistry approach. Once Graphology is mentioned, you'll often find people more than happy to produce the tools you need.

EXAMPLE TWO

You're in a cafe. There's a chatty group of friends (F1, F2, F3) on a nearby table you'd like to get to know. You've been setting the scene by scribbling a few versions of your own signature in a pad for a few minutes. You notice a lull in the group's conversation.

You: (leaning over to the strangers table) **'Hi, sorry to bother you. Can I ask you something?'**

F1: (raising an eyebrow) *'Sure...'*

You: (showing your pad scribbles) *'I'm wondering which signature is best. I've been trying new ones out. I can't tell any more!'*

F1: (as you hand over the pad with pen attached) *'Let's see. Hmm.'*

F2: (leaning over the pad too) *'What's this for anyway? Got a job interview or something?'*

You: *'No, I just read somewhere that changing your signature can also help change your life. I know a bit about Graphology, but I'd never come across that before.'*

F3: *'What's Graphology?'*

F1: *'It's looking at people's handwriting and stuff.'*

You: *'You can tell a lot about someone from their handwriting.'*

F2: (grabbing the pen from the pad) *'Can I take a sheet?'*

You: *'Be my guest.'*

F2: (writing their own signature with a flourish) *'Tada. I'm a freaking genius.'*

F3: (grabbing the pen and sheet for themselves) *'Not sure about that. Here's mine.'*

You: (Stranger 3 scribbles her signature down) *'It's amazing how different everyone's signatures are. Do any of you think of yourselves as a typical male, or typical female? Or do you think you're all completely unique?'*

This example is a good reminder that you should always under-sell your knowledge. You've learnt a thing or two about handwriting, and you'd like to share it with others. Coming across as a a professional can be a barrier to making friends. Keep it light.

> **TOP TIP:** A small golf pencil fits in your pocket, won't leak like a pen, and you can 'discover it' on the floor. It may be fake spontaneity, but it can still get you into position.

G6 Bringing It All Together

Just as we compared the lines of the hand with the fingers during a Palmistry reading, we can compare the Client's typical handwriting with that of their signature. Signatures are generally more flamboyant than handwriting and, seen as a form of artistic expression, can show us how a Client would like to be seen. It is the **typical** sample that represents a Client's true nature, and contrasting this with their signature can be revealing. For many of us, there's no greater contradiction than who we are vs who we want to be, so framing a Graphology reading in this way can generate a lot of interesting conversation.

Graphology Analysis Example

- **Typical: Graphology Golf - Long upwards T shot, dot of the I somewhat high and slightly to the left**

Analysing the word **typical** with Graphology Golf, we can see that the crossing of the T is very high and very long. This would indicate an ambitious and enthusiastic person. We can also see that the dot of the I is somewhat high, and a fraction before the letter itself. If we put these two ideas together, we could say this person has a tendency to overstretch themselves. They may not always reach all their goals, though not from lack of trying.

- **Typical: Sociability / Physicality - Large Y loop but small P loop**

We can see from the large loop in the Y someone who is quite sociable, but from the lack of loop in the P a person who is not so physical.

- **Typical: Slants / Baselines - Leaning forwards, sloping upwards**

The whole word is slanted forward, which compliments the sociable Y, and as it's rising up the page, it indicates an upbeat nature. This compliments the preceding traits.

- **Signature: First letter of first name, second name**

There is only an initial for the Client's first name, yet they have underlined their surname. It appears to be that rather than being sociable and open, this signature is written by someone who is quite formal and likes to present a powerful image of themselves. Also, the signature is not particularly interesting and is perfectly legible. The S, however, is somewhat flamboyant, and shows an artistic flair.

- **Typical vs Signature Comparison**

This Client's signature is a little at odds with their handwriting sample of the word typical:

- The crossing of the T in the signature is far lower than in typical–does the Client have to reign in their normally over-optimistic attitude at work?

- The dot of the I is to the right in the signature, but to the left in typical–is the Client someone who struggles to focus on their goals?

- On a happier note, the signature's baseline rises even more than in typical, suggesting the Client projects even more positivity than at first thought.

Graphology Nutshells

Graphology Golf is almost impossible to forget, the size of the Y and the P loops are easy to judge, and signature analysis comes mainly down to common sense.

Graphology Golf

- Graphology Golf can show us how a Client approaches their goals and ambitions
- The swing is the crossing of the T, the I is the flag and the dot of the I is the golf ball

The size of a Y or P loop indicates how much or little of a trait a Client possesses

- Y - YOU loops show how much of themselves Clients project into the world
- P - PHYSICAL loops shows how physical people are

Handwriting slant suggests a Client's slant on life

- Handwriting slants forward - People that lean towards you find you interesting
- Handwriting slants backward - People that lean away from you are more guarded

Signature names used

- A Client's signature should be viewed as a personal statement
- The names a Client uses in their signature can indicate how formal, informal or serious they are

Signature style

- The style of a signature can indicate how a Client would like to be seen by others
- You can use common sense to interpret a signature's style

GRAPHOLOGY RECAP & QUIZ

Here is a randomised collection of Graphology questions from each recap. It's best to speak all your answers out loud with the quizzes in this book, because even the greatest of answers can be rendered incoherent by one's lips. As always, go back to questions that give you trouble, and run through the quiz several times to make things stick.

Remember these simple rules:

- Graphology Golf is a fun, easy and memorable way to explain the T and the I to a Client

- The loop in the letter Y shows how open You are, and P is for Physical

- Handwriting leans forward to talk, but backwards to withdraw

- Baselines are upbeat when moving up the page, and downbeat when moving down the page

- The names and style a Client uses in their signature reflects on how they'd like to be perceived

THE BIG GRAPHOLOGY QUIZ

Get Your Facts Straight

1. What does a large P loop signify?

2. What does it mean if a Client's handwriting slopes down the page?

3. What could you say about someone who uses their full name in their signature?

4. A Client's handwriting runs straight across the page. What does it mean?

5. What could a small P loop signify?

6. The dot of the I is important. What does it represent?

7. What would a large Y loop signify?

8. What could you say to a Client with a small Y and P loop?

9. How would you describe someone who only used their first name in their signature?

10. In what way is the crossing of the T important?

11. How does the placement of the I dot reflect on a Client's character?

12. What could you say to a Client with a large Y and P loop?

13. What does the letter I signify?

14. What two things could an unreadable signature signify?

15. What does the line that crosses the T signify?

16. What does a small Y loop signify?

17. What could you say about someone who underlined their signature?

18. If a signature only showed a Client's last name, what could it mean?

19. What could it mean if a Client's handwriting leant backwards?

20. What does handwriting that leans neither backwards, nor forwards, signify?

21. If a Client's handwriting rises up the page, what could it mean?

22. What does it mean should a Client's handwriting lean forwards?

23. What could you say about a Client whose signature was a first initial

plus their surname?

24. What does a full stop at the end of a signature signify?

Get Your Mouth In Gear

Explain to each of these Clients what their handwriting and signature say about them. Speak out loud, and in your own words.

25. Marjorie's handwriting sample contains a Small Y loop, and small P loop.

26. Doug's dot of the I seems completely missing.

27. Emily's handwriting slants backwards and runs straight across the page.

28. Laurie's T has been crossed with a large stroke up and to the right, but the dot is placed above the letter I.

29. Ernie's handwriting neither slants forwards nor backwards, and falls down across the page.

30. Louise's signature is tiny, straight and neat, and uses both her first and second names.

31. Brendon's crossing of the T is very short and pointing down, and the dot of the I is high and to the left.

32. Geraldine's signature is a huge squiggle, which looks like it is underlined.

33. Darren's handwriting sample features a Large Y loop, and a small P loop.

34. Augusta's T has a straight, but medium-sized T bar. The dot of the I is not only high, but far over to the right.

35. Kevin uses his full name in his signature, and it is quite large and

flamboyant in style.

36. Leonard's handwriting sample has a Large Y loop, and a large P loop.

37. Pauls's handwriting sample has a Small Y loop, and a large P loop.

38. Gertrude's handwriting slants forwards, and rises up the page significantly.

39. The cross of Cynthia's T is tiny but the dot of the I is perfectly placed, if somewhat high, above the I.

40. Malcolm's handwriting slants backwards significantly, and rises slightly up the page.

41. Johann's signature is nothing more than a tiny squiggle.

42. Colette has underlined her signature, which comprises her surname only. There's little style to it.

G7 Graphology Reading Example

Here's an example reading I could give based on the handwriting sample found on page 195. Unlike Palmistry readings, Graphology readings take some preparation, so I've had a few moments to look over the Client's handwriting. When a Graphology trait is completely at odds with the Client's character, it can be seen as a personal roadblock to their future growth. To illustrate this, I have underlined a section where the Client, a sporty and athletic type, is taken aback when told the lack of a P loop suggests they are physically inactive. At the end of the reading, I refer back to the missing P loop and suggest this as a source of frustration for them.

> **In The James Bond Cold Reading, roadblocks are referred to as waypoints, and you can read about them on page 93.**

'First we'll take a look at the word typical. We can see here from the letter T you have crossed it with a very long upwards stroke. This is a sign of someone who is positive, outgoing and ambitious. If you think of crossing of the letter T a bit like someone taking a swing at a golf ball, this shot would be aiming high and into the distance, don't you think?

'If we look at the dot of the letter I, we can see where the ball actually ended up. As you can see, the dot of your I is also very high, but not quite over the letter I itself. If you imagine that the letter I is the flag where the hole is, you've slightly undershot it. I'd imagine that you are very enthusiastic and put a lot of energy into things, but perhaps you aim too high? I'm not saying you never reach your goals, but perhaps you could reduce the amount you do, and concentrate on the big stuff.

'Let's take a look at the letter P and the letter Y. What we're looking for here are the loops of the letters. You see here, your letter Y has a very large loop. It's pretty easy to remember

what the letter Y means, it's all about YOU. How you present yourself to the world, how outgoing you are, that kind of thing. So this large loop in the letter Y would suggest that you're a very outgoing person, pretty sociable.

'If we look at the loop of the letter P, the letter P is all about physicality. The more of a loop you have the more physical you are. Now you have a letter P with no visible loop whatsoever! Would you agree that you're more sociable than physical? I'm not saying you never do any exercise, I'm just wondering if this makes any sense?

'You think you're pretty active? OK, well that's interesting. You quite like sports and are fairly physical, perhaps we'll find out what that P is all about later. If we look at the way you've written the word 'typical' we can see that it's sloping upwards and is leaning forwards, all traits of a positive upbeat kind of person. So that's the word 'typical', lets take a look at your signature shall we?

'Your signature is interesting as you've written your surname in full but not your first name. I just wondered, do you always write it like that?

'Usually people who don't write their first names are a little bit formal, not exactly shy, but they don't like to give too much away about themselves.

'And here, you've written your surname in full and you've underlined it to make a point. That is the sign of a strong character! Perhaps you've had to fight for what you want when it comes to work, or you have to put a formal face on when you do business?

'So this is interesting. Although you're outgoing and highly sociable, you have this slight distance you put between yourself and others.

'So although we're trying to see if you're a typical male /

female, you have this high drive to achieve and appear to have the demeanour to go through with it all. I'm still confused about this physical P loop though. Have you had any injuries in the past?

'It's strange because sometimes people's handwriting changes as they evolve, sometimes it can even reflect their lives. Perhaps you need to stop working so much and give yourself more time to follow the sports and activities you enjoy, as the lack of a P loop could show some kind of physical frustration.

If we look at the dot of the I in your signature, we can see that it's high once again, but this time it slightly overshoots the hole in our imaginary golf game. Perhaps you get things done by sheer willpower, even in the face of adversity!'

A few notes on this example:

- Graphology Golf is the best way to kick off a reading. It is a lot of fun, making it easy to remember for both you and the Client.

- I pause often as I report my findings to the Client, and give them ample chance to respond.

- I use contradictions to fuel conversation. In this example, I suggest the no-loop-P suggests the Client could be physically frustrated somehow, no matter how active they are.

- Should a Client be unreceptive, bring proceedings to a swift close. A brief explanation of Graphology Golf can be enough for some people.

> **TOP TIP:** Different oracles have different feels to them. Compare this example reading to the Palmistry example, and consider the ways each oracle may feel different to a Client.

G8 Graphology Reading Practice

Get Your Mouth In Gear #1

Highlight the various traits shown in these typical handwriting examples, as if explaining each trait to a Client. Speak out loud as you go, but don't worry too much about giving readings just yet. Simply focus on spotting as many individual traits as you can in each example.

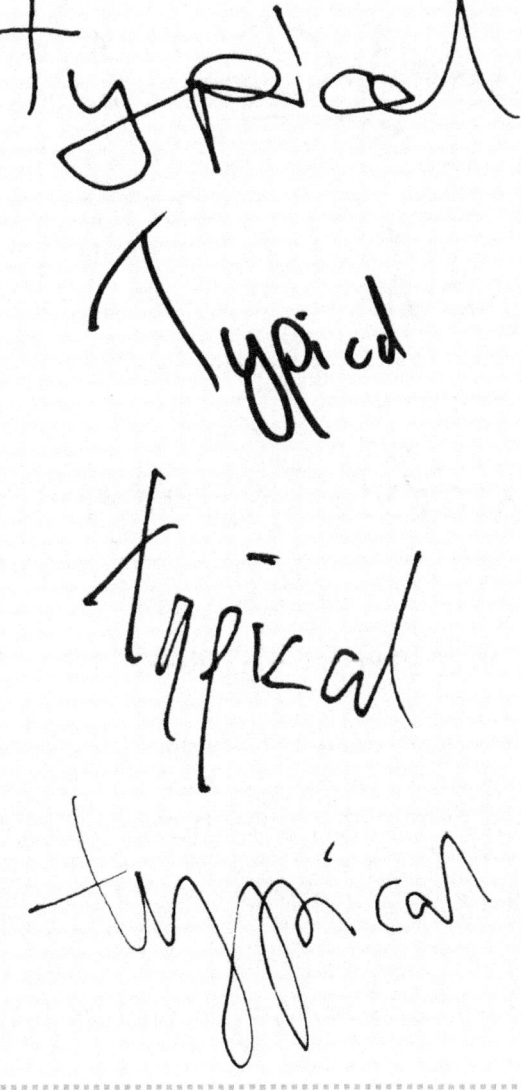

Come up with one sentence that could describe each of these signatures to their owner.

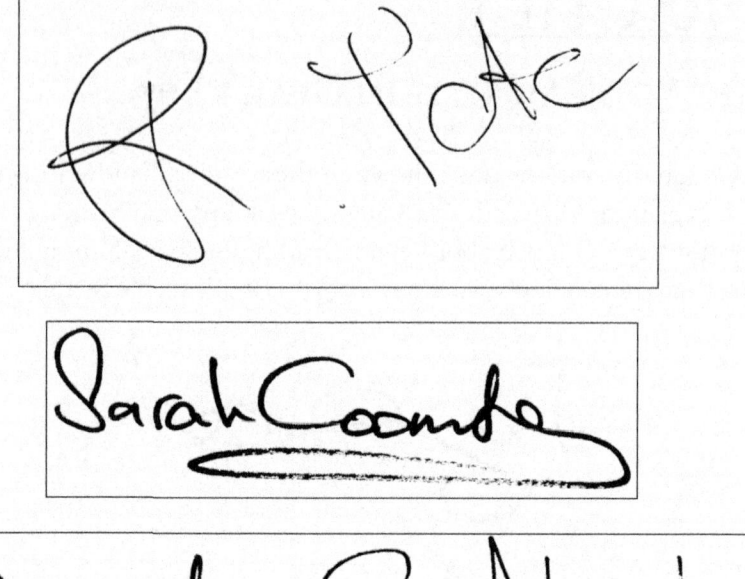

···

GET YOUR MOUTH IN GEAR #2

Give each of these Clients a reading based on the handwriting examples above, considering each Client's gender, age and background. Speak out loud as if they were in front of you, and try to talk for as long as you can.

Benjamin, Male, 16–Last year of school, mop of hair, band t-shirt, hates their parents

Diana, Female, 55–Thinking of retirement, dyed hair, flowery dress, health issues

Wilbur, Male, 28–Recently married, short tidy hair, casual smart, sporty and proud

Sigrid, Female, 30–Wants children, long curly hair, jeans and a top, loud and intense

To create each graphology reading, you will need to combine both the typical and signature examples together. Pair these with each Client in order initially, but also try mixing and matching the examples, noticing how much or how little each reading can change with different combinations.

G9 Graphology Conclusion

Graphology is, in many ways, a safer bet than Palmistry. Not all situations are appropriate for the touchy–feely vibe of a palm reading and, free from the negative connotations associated with fortune telling, Graphology works well with couples and groups. Graphology is also widely accepted as a social science and, thanks to a proliferation of detective dramas in both film and television, is perceived as an acceptable branch of forensic research. There are very few situations where there is no pen or paper to hand, and even if you only get as far as Graphology Golf with a Client, I urge you to try it. Don't forget that many of the concepts found in the Palmistry chapter can enhance a Graphology reading so, whether you are drawn to Palmistry or not, it's still worth reading.

If you have enjoyed the Graphology method outlined here and want to take things a step further, please check out my book **'Graphology - The Art Of Handwriting Analysis'**. The book adds to the Golf Analogy and the meanings of the letters Y and P, but uses a memorable two-word phrase rather than the seven letters from the word typical. A set of digital flash cards accompany the book, and these can be downloaded, free of charge, from my website. They work great when printed on index cards, or you can upload them to your phone or tablet for digital viewing.

A tick sheet is also available for the book from my website, cleverly named **'Graphology Tick Sheet'**. Tick sheets serve both as a memory aid for you, the reader, and as a souvenir for Clients. If you want to take your Graphology readings to the next level, the tick sheet is a great next step.

May happiness be the signature of your life!

www.coldreading.co

5
NUMEROLOGY

Although people often choose numbers in their lives based on those they believe bring the most luck, Numerology readings focus on the one number that cannot be chosen nor changed; a person's birth date. Unfortunately, asking a stranger for their date of birth is not the best way to strike up a conversation and, as people grow older, their willingness to reveal their age diminishes. For Clients in their twenties, this is not a problem, but for some in their mid-thirties and beyond, revealing one's age to a complete stranger can be problematic.

To avoid the chances of getting pulled into an uneasy guess-the-age scenario, we will be using the digits from a Client's mobile phone number as the basis for a Numerology reading. A mobile phone number is the holy grail of contact details, and a reading based on its digits is an unusual idea that grabs people's attention. The concept is that, as the number is relatively recent, its permutations can offer a better glimpse into a Client's immediate present than a traditional reading. To make things more personal and less random, we will be throwing the Client's lucky number into the mix.

To give a Numerology reading, you need a basic understanding of the meanings of the numbers one through nine. Nine meanings for nine numbers may appear daunting, but the system explained here is designed to be memorable. The meanings are woven into a story to give them context, and each number has a helpful memory peg attached. The number four, for instance, can be thought of as a square denoting the security of a house, and you will not be surprised to learn that one and two represent beginnings and cooperation, respectively. The meanings attributed to each digit tend to be self-explanatory, and stem from traditional Numerology concepts.

N1 Number Meanings

This section deals exclusively with the meanings of the numbers one through ten. You'll find a fair amount of repetition in the next few pages, but hopefully this slicing and dicing of information can help give you a better chance of retention. Read this section a handful of times, and you should be good to go.

Take your time when reading through the following number meanings. Ask yourself how you might go about committing the meaning of each number to memory. See if you can think of any rhymes, shapes, or catchphrases that could help connect each number to their meaning. Try not to move to the next number until you have come up with at least one good idea that could help commit the current number meaning to memory.

Basic Meanings

1. Beginnings
2. Cooperation
3. Expansion
4. Security
5. Activity
6. Communication
7. Spirituality
8. Inspiration
9. Changes
10. Success

It can help if you imagine the numbers on a ten-hour clock, the number 10 being the realisation of all that the 1 can be. This is analogous to not only the many eras of our lives, such as school, career and parenthood, but of our entire life cycle from birth to death. Making it to a ripe old age is, in itself, a success story.

N2 Life Cycle Basics

Let's bring the numbers to life by adding some context. Visualising the numbers as a Life Cycle makes them less abstract and, as each stage leads organically to the next, easier to remember. The hope is that, through visualisation, the thought of any one digit will conjure up an assortment of ideas, concepts and images we can use in our Numerology reading.

Here are the basics of the Life Cycle, split into three sections. The overarching concept is that of birth till success in adulthood, rather than birth till death, with 10 signifying the realisation of dreams and the start of a new cycle. It should be noted that the concept of birth does not occur until the number three, the numbers one and two representing the coming together of two people to create a third.

- We all begin alone, we couple up, and bring life into the world before we make a home with four walls.

- There is much activity as the child grows, and before long, the child learns to communicate, and asks big questions about the world around them.

- Finally, they are inspired to go out into the world, make a difference, and be successful. They are now alone, and the cycle can begin again.

Read these three sentences through a few times to familiarise yourself with the basic cycle. See if you can attribute a number to each concept before reading further.

> **Using a story to link the meanings of the digits 1 to 9 is a technique similar to that used in the James Bond Cold Reading. Should you wish, you can use any digit from a Numerology readings to remind you of a corresponding JBCR line.**

Here's the sequence again, with each number and meaning indicated at the relevant point in the cycle.

- We all begin alone (1: Beginnings) we couple up (2: Cooperation) and bring life into the world (3: Expansion) before we make a home with four walls (4: Security)

- There is much activity as the child grows (5: Activity) and before long the child learns to communicate (6: Communication) and asks big questions about the world around them (7: Spirituality).

- Finally, they are inspired to go out into the world (8: Inspiration) to make a difference (9: Changes) and be successful (10: Success). They are now alone (1: Beginnings) and the cycle begins again.

Numbers are, by definition, all about progression. Things start, and they end. I am sure you can see why lower digits signify ideas and planning, whereas higher numbers allude to a final push for success.

In the next section we'll run through the story again in greater detail. You don't have to commit these descriptions to memory, but you have to give them some thought. As each number is a journey on a path rather than an isolated concept, you'll have a better chance of relaying their meanings to a Client once you understand the sequence.

IMAGINE

Once you have read each number's description, sit with the number and its ideas for a while before moving to the next. See if you can think of anything personal that could help cement the meaning of each number in your mind. No matter how old you are, try to imagine yourself in each stage of the cycle by adding elements of your past (and possibly, a future you would like for yourself) into each visualisation.

N3 Life Cycle In Detail

1 The Power Of One - I Stand Alone - Beginnings
The number 1 looks like a capital I, as in Me, Myself and I

We have to start somewhere, and a blank canvas affords a great deal of energy and optimism. We're number one! We could be starting from scratch, or starting again (coming full circle). There is no fear, and anything's possible. This number one is not about knowing you have arrived, it is about knowing you could get there if you put your mind to it. It is the optimism and naivety of a teenager who's willing to try anything, free from habits and preconceived notions. This number one is a healthy selfish, not the kind that crushes other people but one that drags others along with an optimistic, and somewhat idealistic, outlook. The only downside is that this boundless energy can lack direction and tends to fizzle without focus.

2 Me And You - Two's Company - Cooperation
Two swans touching beaks form a heart silhouette.

Most people do not stay single forever. We meet someone and fall in love, and caring for others forces our ego to take a back seat. We learn to share. We learn to cooperate and learn to work as part of a team. Compromise is not always easy, but two minds are better than one and the rewards can be substantial. We see the world through another person's eyes and learn to appreciate their point of view. We also form partnerships in our professional lives, as well as those closer to home.

3 We Create Life - Three's A Crowd - Expansion
The number 3 looks like a pair of breasts to feed a baby.

Only two people can bring a third person into the world. Three signifies the growth of something from nothing, and the fruits of cooperation. There may be labour pains, but the rewards are great. Even business partners refer to their companies as their babies. The number three is about seeing things come to life as they grow beyond a mere concept.

4 We Make A Home - Four Walls - Security
A square has four sides, a house shape with square windows and doors.

When a new baby arrives, parents seek stability in the four walls of house and home for their family. Structure and order, alongside safety and practicality, are required. Although much needs to be done, there is a sense of settling down combined with the initial flush of achievement. For many people, a happy home with children is a life-goal, making the number four the end of a cycle. Kids or not, four represents the solid foundation required for any plans and growth.

5 The Family Grows - Five Alive - Activity
Five is a hive of activity!

The transition from baby to child can be pretty hectic. There is always something to do and plans to make, and children never look back. Life seems to go at twice the speed, everything seems to happen at once, and multi-tasking is the order of the day. There are various types of growth, both physical and mental but, no matter how out-of-control things feel, there is no turning back. Five is not like the number three, which creates something from nothing, but the speedy development of things that are already there.

6 The Child Learns To Communicate - 6 Is Social - Communication
The number 6 looks like an eye, or an ear, or a telephone.

Before long, the child communicates with the world and people around them. Personal interaction, plus a need to be understood, are the order of the day. A child may attempt to communicate with sounds, looks and actions, their building blocks and scribbles. The number six is about connecting with people on a deeper level than a text message or an email.

7 The Child Asks Big Questions - Seventh Heaven - Spirituality
The number 7 looks like a question mark.

Once a child can communicate sufficiently, they ask difficult questions for which adults rarely have the answer. 'Where did I come from?' is a typical query from an infant, yet it is one many of us repeat throughout our lifetimes. The need to ask big questions has a spiritual ring to it, and we would all like to know where we truly came from, how we got to where we are, and what it is all about. Seven is about looking up to the heavens for divine inspiration.

8 The Child Is Inspired To Leave Home - Eight Through The Gate - Inspiration
8 looks like a lightbulb illuminating the moment inspiration strikes.

The eight is about leaving home for good, taking our first strides towards adulthood as we forge our own path. The number eight is as much about inspiration as perspiration and requires the determination to follow ideas through. A leap of faith is required, the kind that propels young adults to leave home.

9 They Make A Difference - Plan Nine (From Outer Space) - Changes
The number 9 is the activity before the success of 10/10. Like 6, the number 9 also looks like eye, ear, telephone, but this time it is on a higher more adult level of communication and action fuelled by determination and knowledge.

Once we head out into the world, we learn that progress requires change, both internally and externally. We need to learn to adapt to the world, even if we mean to change it for the better. Major life milestones demand that we leave a part of our older selves behind in order to get ahead, so nine represents the final, often ruthless, push to become a better, wiser, and more successful version of ourselves. Everything is going to plan, so the sky's the limit!

10 They Become Successful - Ten Out Of Ten - Success

Top marks, the realisation of a goal or dream. The end of one cycle and the beginning of another.

What was once a child is now a fully formed adult in their own right. Ten represents top marks and high accomplishment earned through the other nine stages. The number ten has two digits rather than one and a zero has appeared! The zero is a spark of an idea that a new cycle could start again. At the end of any cycle, we are left thinking, now what? Success can be short-lived, and the next day arrives just like any other, as we turn our attention to new challenges and experiences.

STOP RIGHT NOW!

You now know enough about Numerology to start a conversation.

Numerology can feel overwhelming at first. However, you do not need every digit's meaning under your belt to start a conversation, and a few choice numbers are more than enough to get talking. Although we have not covered mobile phone readings yet, you can still discuss numbers without a reading system in place. In the right situation, you can at least ask whether certain numbers crop up in a Client's life and, should they divulge their birthdate, tell them something about what their numbers say about them.

For instance, you may find you can easily recall the numbers 1 to 3, dealing with new beginnings, partnerships and expansion, and the number 8, because you find the lightbulb moment easy to remember. If this is the case, there is no harm discussing these numbers alone, and admitting openly you are unsure of the rest. As always, you're not claiming to be an expert, so in the interests of starting a conversation, it's better to discuss what you know, rather than worrying about what you do not. Encouraging Clients to help fill the gaps in your knowledge can come across as both humble and engaging, two qualities you most definitely want to develop on your journey as a reader.

You can read more about how to get things going in The Approach section of this chapter.

In A Nutshell

1 and 10 signify beginnings and endings, the thrill of new ventures and the satisfaction of completion.

2 for cooperation makes perfect sense as in love, balance, and the coming together of two people.

3 for expansion comes from two people creating a third, of concepts made real and the fruits of labour.

4 for stability are the four walls of the family home, solid foundations for a child to develop.

5 is for the growth and activity in the home itself, a hive bursting with life, the dot in the centre of a 5 die.

6 for communication, the 6 looks like an eye, an ear and a telephone.

7 for the spiritual seventh heaven, in the shape of a question mark.

8 is out of the gate, when you are getting out there to seek your fortune and…

9 is the final push for victory, the last mile, and everything finally coming together.

10 is the successful outcome, the realisation of everything that has gone before, the end of one cycle and the start of another.

LIFE CYCLE RECAP 1

See if you can answer these questions before you move on.

Get Your Facts Straight

1. How will you remember what the number 4 signifies?

2. What does 8 rhyme with?

3. 10 signifies success, but what else can it mean?

4. The number 6 looks like several things to help you remember its meaning. What are they?

5. Why do you think the number 2 signifies love?

6. How can the number 2 help us remember the significance of the number 3?

7. This is the number 7. It looks curious, but what does it rhyme with?

8. The number 1 is closely tied to the number 10. But why?

9. The number 5 rhymes with something that buzzes. What is it?

10. 9 is very nearly a 10. How can that help us remember its meaning?

N4 Life Cycle Chapters

Let's break the life cycle into three chapters again, adding what we've learnt so far.

1-3 : I Stand Alone / Two's Company / Three's A Crowd
The first three numbers are about fresh starts and early development

The numbers 1-3 have their own little story. A single person (1) meets someone (2) and they have a baby together (3). When you're a single young adult (1), life is all about excitement and trying new things out with great enthusiasm. Then you meet someone (2) and share your life with them. Then (sometimes!) you have a baby (3) and you've both made a new number one!

I Stand Alone, Two's Company & Three's A Crowd are well-known sayings and perfectly illustrate what each number means.

4-7 : These Four Walls / 5 Alive / 6 Is Social / 7th Heaven
Numbers four to seven are to do with early childhood and personal growth

Security is needed, so a house (4) is built for the family to live in. The baby grows into a child (5), introducing the frenetic activity that revolves around bringing up kids. The child learns to communicate (6) and becomes a member of society. As the child develops, they ask bigger questions (7) as they approach adulthood.

These Four Walls represent the security required for growth, enabling the rapid development from baby to child in Five Alive. Six Is Social is about outgrowing the physical confines of These Four Walls, and 7th Heaven is about outgrowing a family's inherited thoughts and ideas.

8-10 : Eight Through The Gate / Plan 9 / Ten Out Of Ten
These last numbers are more to do with adulthood and achievement

Finally, the young adult leaves home (8) to make their way in the world. There is a need to make things happen (9), and their involvement outside of the family home shapes and changes that world. They can finally stand on their own two feet and realise their dreams (10). The cycle ends to begin again, with a new number one to start a fresh cycle.

Eight Through The Gate is about leaving home, and Plan Nine is about making plans and following dreams in the real world. Ten Out Of Ten is the satisfaction that comes from realising those dreams.

In A Nutshell

Here is a table showing the number meanings, phrases and visuals together. Not only is this a useful reference, it is a good way to test yourself on each number's meaning.

MEANING	PHRASE	VISUAL
1. Beginnings	1 Stand Alone	Me, Myself and 1
2. Cooperation	2's Company	2 swans = heart silhouette
3. Expansion	3's A Crowd	3 = breasts to feed a baby
4. Security	4 Walls	A house has 4 walls
5. Activity	5 Alive	5 is a hive of activity
6. Communication	6 Is Social	6 = eye, ear or telephone
7. Spirituality	7th Heaven	7 is a question mark
8. Inspiration	8 The Gate	8 is a lightbulb
9. Changes	Plan 9	9 is a higher level 6
10. Success	10 Out Of 10	You aced it!

LIFE CYCLE RECAP 2
See if you can answer these questions before you move on

Get Your Facts Straight

1. 6 is Social, but what three things does the number 6 look like?

2. What object has 4 Walls?

3. Which number makes you think of a lightbulb moment?

4. Which two numbers represent success and new beginnings?

5. The 6 changes to a 9 once inverted. How is that significant?

6. The numbers 2 and 3 can be remembered using a pair of well-known phrases. What are they?

7. What number do you think of when you imagine a bee returning home?

8. Only one digit resembles a question mark. Which is it?

Get Your Mouth In Gear

9. Someone asks you the difference between the meanings of the numbers 1, 2 and 3. What could you say to them?

10. You are teaching some basic Numerology to a friend. What could you say to help them learn the meanings of the numbers 4 to 7 in the shortest possible time, using the rhymes you have learnt in this chapter?

11. Whilst studying this book together, your partner admits they do not quite understand the differences between the number eight and the number nine. How could you explain each number's meaning using the last third of the life cycle?

12. Give a mini lecture on the numbers 1 through 9 as if talking to a group of students. Use the life cycle story to your advantage, and talk openly about each number for as long as you can. Refer to this book as little as possible should you get stuck, and try to keep talking no matter how lost for words you feel. Fake it till you make it.

> **TOP TIP:** Pulling cards randomly from a shuffled deck of cards, with the face cards removed, is a good way to practice the recall of Numerology meanings. Toss cards to one side whose numbers you struggle with, and give them a little more thought later.

N5 Mobile Number Readings

Mobile Number Readings are based mainly on the digits of a Client's mobile number. The concept is that, as mobile numbers are relatively recent entries in a Client's life, their digits can reveal the numerical forces working both for and against a Client. Unlike Palmistry or Graphology, Numerology deals with a Client's life-trends rather than their character, although their personality is revealed as the reading unfolds. You must highlight and encourage the Client to take advantage of, and overcome, any opportunities or obstacles that come to light.

One more number is required to give a Mobile Number Reading–the lucky number of the Client. If they don't have a lucky number, their current house or flat number can be used, as can any other number they deem relevant. Asking whether a particular number has reoccurred in their life can help jog their memory, and you will find many Clients have lived at the same house number more than once. Although these numbers are not exactly lucky, they are at least relevant to the Client.

Through simple observation, you can tell a lot about a Client before any mention of Mobile Number Readings, so use your common sense and pick up what you can. Some people know their mobile number off by heart. Others may have never learnt them at all. Those that know their number may use it frequently for business, or have a busy social life. Clients with a new phone (or one buried deep in their bag) may have no clue at all about their number. Similarly, Client's attitudes towards their phones can be useful, and you can tell a lot about a Client from their brand of phone, its current state and from the cover they may use to protect it. The topic of phones is a great way to start a conversation and, when pushed about phone use, friends may blame each other for never answering and / or wasting time on social media.

As Mobile Number Reading require knowledge of a Client's lucky number, we're going to talk about how to approach a potential Client *before* delving into the mechanics of giving a Numerology reading.

N6 The Approach

This section is about drawing people into a conversation about Numerology

The easiest way to prompt a Numerology reading is to bring up the subject of lucky numbers, as many people feel a certain number has followed them through their lives. For instance, the number 36 has cropped up several times in my life (school number, house number etc) and for this reason, I've always considered it my lucky number. Once a Client's lucky number has been established, the idea can be proposed to use both their mobile phone number, and their lucky number, as the basis for a Numerology reading. Most Clients will be happy to tell you their lucky number but, although some numbers are based on joyful events such as wedding dates, they are often derived from the birthdays of deceased loved ones. Lucky numbers are rarely frivolous, and some numbers are chosen for extremely personal reasons, so tread carefully.

Similar to Graphology readings, an easy way to segue into a Mobile Number Reading is to start with a bit of Palmistry. This idea is covered in the Graphology approach section, but rather than switching from the lines of a Client's hand to their signature, you ask whether they have a lucky number. Once that's established, it's easy to progress into a Mobile Number Reading.

If the Palmistry angle feels inappropriate, you will need to seek other opportunities. Luckily, there are numbers to be found everywhere in day-to-day life, but the trick is to highlight numbers that appear sufficiently relevant to a potential Client to create conversation. Some numbers will be personally relevant, whereas others will be more circumstantial to a Client. You'll still to need to write it all down of course so, like impromptu Graphology readings, you'll need to rustle up a pen and paper from somewhere.

> **TOP TIP:** Numerology can stray into fortune-telling if you're not careful, so focus on personal development rather than chances of winning the lottery.

Personal Numbers

Any number that seems personal to a potential Client can fuel a conversation.

A   Social birthdays, featuring cards and possibly balloons with numbers
B   Tattoos and jewellery that feature dates and numbers
C   Numbers on t-shirts and other clothing

Birthday celebrations featuring cards and balloons are a soft conversational target, and relieve the embarrassment of asking people's ages. Some people's tattoos, jewellery and even clothes feature dates and numbers.

- Does potential Client A understand the opportunities hidden in their latest age number?
- Are the numbers in Client B's tattoos and jewellery more significant than they realise?
- Could Client C be persuaded that the numbers on their t-shirt are less arbitrary than they appear?

Circumstantial Numbers

Any numbers crossing a potential Client's path in the present moment can fuel a conversation.

D   Numbers on book and magazine covers
E   Table numbers / bar numbers in pubs and restaurants
F   Numbers in artwork and other surroundings

A book a potential Client is reading may have numbers in its title, such as Twelfth Night or Fahrenheit 451. There may be several numbers on the book of a potential Client's magazine, such as those found on the cover of Sudoku puzzle books. Some pubs have numbered tables for food orders, and some hand out numbered spoons once an order at the bar is made. Numbers also appear on posters and decorative art in pubs and restaurants.

- Has potential Client D considered that Four Past Midnight may have been an interesting book choice?
- Could potential Client's E's table number be relevant to them in some way?
- Did potential Client F understand the significance of sitting beneath a film poster for Catch 22?

It's impossible to list every situation here and of course, no two environments, nor potential Clients, are the same. Many of these scenarios may seem absurd, but you never know what will work and what won't. It's hard to deny that, in the right setting, with the right people, when the mood feels upbeat and there's nothing else to lose, some of these tactics will be successful conversation starters. At worst, you will appear eccentric, but at best you will pique people's interest enough to get them talking to you. Crazy or not, these ideas beat the dead-end tactic of asking a stranger the time by a significant margin.

Your Lucky Number

We have discussed how you can leverage both a potential Client's personal, and circumstantial numbers, to start a Numerology conversation. What we have not mentioned is how your own lucky number can be useful, especially when you invent one to suit the situation. This may be sneaky, but it certainly makes your approach more relevant. Instead of asking a potential Client what a number means to them, you can turn the tables, and tell them what it means to you.

A   35 years old? That's my lucky number. Do you have a lucky number?
B   I've no idea what your tattoo signifies, but 21 is my lucky number. I hope it brings you luck too!
C   Cool t-shirt. Is 15 your lucky number or something? It is mine. Do you know what it means?
D   That's my lucky number, perhaps I should read that book. Is it yours too?
E   Damn, you're sat at my table. That's my lucky number. Hope I don't get food poisoning...
F   You're sat right under my lucky number. Hope it brings you luck. Would you like to know what it means?

Again, these examples will not work with everybody, but they illustrate the creative headspace needed to pull a conversation out of thin air. As always, remember to have fun and to keep things lighthearted.

THE GROUP APPROACH

Approach example two in the Graphology section discussed a scenario in a cafe where a group of friends were tasked with picking your best signature from a selection. We can't quite use numbers in the same way, but we can ask a group of people whether a circumstantial number, such as the table number they are seated at in a cafe, is relevant to them somehow. Relevant or not, a quick description of the number's meaning can lead swiftly onto the idea of Mobile Number Readings, and whether it was fortuitous for any of these strangers to be sitting where they are sitting.

You: (walking past) *'Damn, you're sat at my table.'*

Stranger 1: *'What do you mean?'*

You: (stopping to chat) *'The number 9 means success. Has anyone ever lived at a flat or house number 9?'*

Stranger 2: *'I lived at a 39 once, it's my mums old house number.'*

You: *'That's interesting. The number 9 is really lucky. I'm not sure if I remember rightly, but the number 3 is all about new things. Were you born there?'*

Stranger 2: *'No, I was born in the hospital. But yes, pretty much.'*

You: *'You should always look out for number 9s. I always try to pick a mobile number with a lot of 9s in it.'*

Stranger 2: (to Stranger 3) *'Your numbers got a lot of 9s in it.'*

Stranger 3: *'994 9836... yeah you're right. Lucky me!'*

You: *'Does anyone have a lucky number?'*

Stranger 4: *'23, it was my grandma's birthday on the 23rd.'*

You: *'Are there any 2s and 3s in your mobile number? The number 2 is all about partnerships.'*

Stranger 2: *'And the 3 is about new things.'*

You: *'You're catching on...'*

Stranger 4: (concentrating) *'Nope, no 2s or 3s in my mobile number.'*

You: *'That's a shame. It sounds like you need more 2s and 3s in your life! Anyway, best of luck.'*

Stranger 1: *'Hey, come back a second. What about my number, it's 01138 299145...'*

This is just an example, and things rarely go this smoothly. However, through sheer persistence, you'll get the occasional approach that goes undeniably well. You've got to be in it to win it.

Other Approaches

- 'Does anyone know their own mobile number off by heart these days? My mum can never remember hers, and when I asked my brother the other day, he could only remember his old one.'

- 'Can anyone remember a phone number from years ago, back in the day when you had to remember this kind of thing? I can still remember my old landline from when I was a kid. Anyone else?'

- 'Sometimes you get given a number, but sometimes your provider gives you the chance to choose a number from a list. Some numbers are better than others, right? Have any of you picked your own number like this?'

N7 Bringing It All Together

It's all very well knowing the meanings of the numbers one through nine, but a Numerology reading needs some simple calculations, called a Number Chart, to keep things interesting. There's something vaguely theatrical about creating new numbers from old, and to a Client the process can feel both revealing and rewarding. It's worth taking the time to explain what you're doing when setting up a Number Chart, so take it slowly, and reveal the final numbers with a flourish. The Client won't really know what is going on, but it's worth using the process to build a sense of anticipation and excitement.

The best way to explain the mechanics of a Mobile Phone Reading is via an example. We will explain the system through this example Number Chart, whilst commenting on what could be said to the Client.

The Number Chart

Each mobile number has a prefix particular to their specific network. For instance, in the UK the prefix for the 02 network is 07545. Only the second half of the number, six digits at the time of writing, is unique to the network, and it is these six numbers we use to create a reading. For instance, for the phone number 07545 123456 we ignore the 07545 entirely and concentrate solely on the digits 123456.

To start the reading, we're going to need the last six digits of the Client's mobile number, alongside their lucky number. As an example, we're going to use the mobile phone number 07595 326485 and the lucky number 36.

Firstly, copy down the Client's full mobile number 07595 326485. You then cross through the network prefix, leaving you with 326485.

$$\cancel{07595}\ 326485$$

You then draw a line beneath this remaining number and write the Client's lucky number below, creating a fraction.

$$\frac{326485}{36}$$

You now execute an extremely common Numerology technique, that of distilling each row of numbers down to their base number. You do this by repeatedly adding the digits in each row together until you are left with only one digit or the number 10. As you now know, 10 has its own meaning separate from the single digit 1.

In this example, we add the six digits of the mobile number together 3 + 2 + 6 + 4 + 8 + 5 = 28. As this 28 is still two digits long, we repeat the process, adding add the 2 and the 8 together. We are left with 10, and we stop. If the Client's lucky number is over two digits long, we process it in the same way. Here, we add the 3 and the 6, giving us 9.

$$\frac{326485}{36} = \frac{28}{9} = \frac{10}{9}$$

In this example, the mobile number took two attempts to distill it down to its base number 10. Even though the lucky number took only one attempt, the 9 is carried over so that the mobile number can resolve to 10. If the Client's lucky number was 9 in the first place, the reading would have had three 9s at its base.

The top number 10 of the final result is the Client's Destiny Number, and its meaning shows the prevailing trend in their life at this time. The bottom digit 9 is the Client's Lucky Root, whose meaning shows a longer life trend, based as it is on their own lucky number.

Finally, we calculate the Client's Number Of Opportunity by taking the smallest number in the final fraction away from the largest number (in this case, taking the Lucky Root 9 away from the Destiny Number 10). This number is one the Client should look out for as they head into the future.

$$\begin{array}{lr}\textit{DESTINY} & \underline{10} \\ \textit{LUCKY ROOT} & \underline{9} \\ \textit{OPPORTUNITY} & 1\end{array}$$

(HIGHEST MINUS LOWEST 10-9)

Before we look at giving a reading from this Client's number chart, let's take a slightly closer look at each digit and what it represents, alongside some brief comments on the example.

Destiny Number

The Destiny Number highlights current background forces in the Client's life, using a number that has only recently come into play.

- We know that the number 10 is all about success, so there may be a current of success flowing through the Client's life at the moment. The 10 is also the end of a cycle, so it may signify the end of an era.

Lucky Root

The Lucky Root highlights the overall background forces in the Client's life, using a number that has been in play for a substantial period.

- The number 9 deals with success, but also the changes demanded from the end of a cycle. This could indicate a prevailing trend of optimism throughout the Client's life, but also of pushing themselves too hard.

Number Of Opportunity

The Number Of Opportunity highlights the future ideas and concepts that could help the Client.

- The number 1 is all about new beginnings and fresh starts, so it could be that they need to concentrate on wrapping up their current cycle to start afresh. Bearing the previous numbers in mind, they may want to look out for new opportunities in their life.

Explaining the meanings of these numbers to the Client in sequence forms the basis of a Mobile Phone Reading. Similar to Palmistry and Graphology readings, we need to compare the numbers and their meanings with the help of the Client, seeking as many contradictions as we can to create conversation. To give the Client as much chance of relating to each number as possible, you will need to explain each number fully, using the Numerology meanings given. Like any other reading, you'll need to leave long pauses, and to look out for signs indicating a positive or negative response to your descriptions.

If time is short, you can give a brief reading using just these three numbers. However, three numbers can raise more questions than they answer, so here are a few techniques to extend the reading.

Resonant Numbers

You can view the numbers in the reading as covering the Client's life up to the present day, the numbers to the left being in the past and the final calculation being the present. One could argue that the reading should only cover the time since the Client got a new mobile number, but to keep things simple (and to prevent getting sidetracked) it's best not mention this unless specifically asked. If the Client has a relatively new mobile number, take advantage of the situation by giving a reading based solely on the period from when it came into their possession. You can even give a reading based on their old number too and compare both readings.

Although this left-to-right approach can help extend a reading, things get a lot more interesting when we add the concept of resonant numbers.

Resonant Numbers are digits that repeat in a reading and have special significance. For instance, if we look at the example reading from beginning to end, there are two 2s, two 3s, two 6s and two 9s. Underlining repeating numbers can help us spot their frequency more easily, whilst bringing them to the attention of the Client as we explain what we see.

$$\frac{3\underline{26}485}{\underline{36}} = \frac{\underline{2}8}{\underline{9}} = \frac{10}{\underline{9}}$$

If we combine the concept of resonant numbers with the idea of a left-to-right reading, we can give these influences some kind of time frame.

2 - Cooperation

The resonant number 2 indicates a background of cooperation, appearing early in the reading, as well as mid-way through. This could indicate cooperation of some kind over the last few years until fairly recently.

3 - Expansion

The resonant 3s, both appearing to the far left of the reading, represent expansion. This would indicate a wave of activity at the start of the Client's current cycle. The number 3 doesn't appear anywhere else but the start, so does this mean the adventure is over?

6 - Communication

The resonant 6 shows communication, and these 6s appear early in the reading. Perhaps communication has become less important as time goes on, or has been lost altogether.

9 - Changes

At the far end of the reading we have two 9s, putting an even greater emphasis on success, and a build up to change.

Absent Numbers

Digits missing from the reading are called absent numbers, and can show us which influences are lacking in a Client's life. These can be things a

Client would like more of, such as the romance of 2 or the security of 4, so absent numbers are great for switching the conversation to those things the Client would like to attract.

In our example, there is only one digit missing, the 7 of spirituality. Spirituality can mean various things to various people, from a need to connect with nature to devout religious practice. This brings up the important point that you have no way of telling whether any number trend is a good, or bad thing, for the Client. Only the Client can tell you how they feel about any number, absent or not, so the best you can do is empower them to overcome, or embrace, what is there. To some, a missing 7 may indicate a religious crisis, but to others, it may mean nothing at all. You are simply the messenger, so let the Client decide how each number affects them personally, and work from there.

In the example given, a missing 7 could show that, after a sustained period of successful career growth, the Client's spiritual side has fallen to the wayside. Now a new cycle is starting, should they spend more time on nurturing their pastimes, and those things they care more deeply about? Perhaps they need to get back on track with a certain religious practice they felt benefitted them in the past, or they need more time in the great outdoors. You can offer suggestions like this throughout the reading, but only the Client knows how they feel. The more they can verbalise their own answers, the better, but some Client's need more help to express themselves than others.

Give the Client time to draw their own conclusions as you talk through each number meaning. When they have questions, seek numbers that may have the answers. If they look confused, try explaining a number differently. Encourage the Client to speak openly about what it could all mean but, rather than letting them feel helpless, instil in them the idea they have the power to change and overcome whatever they may see. Steer the reading towards personal growth rather than random acts of God, and never predict anything outside the sphere of the Client. Shed new light on the Client's life, and give them the confidence to tackle whatever is thrown at them.

Unlike the Palmistry and Graphology reading examples, I've not had to worry too much about contradictions in this Numerology example.

Numerology Nutshells

The following Numerology nutshells contain everything you need to give a Mobile Phone Reading. Use it as a reference and come back to it often, especially when starting out. A quick glance can be all that it takes to jog your memory, so copy it down or take a quick snap on your phone for later study.

Numerology 1 to 10

1 and 10 signify beginnings and endings, the thrill of new ventures and the satisfaction of completion.

2 for cooperation makes perfect sense as in love, balance, and the coming together of two people.

3 for expansion comes from two people creating a third, of concepts made real and the fruits of labour.

4 for stability are the four walls of the family home, solid foundations for a child to develop.

5 is for the growth and activity in the home itself, a hive bursting with life, the dot in the centre of a 5 die.

6 for communication, the 6 looks like an eye, an ear and a telephone.

7 for the spiritual seventh heaven, in the shape of a question mark.

8 is out of the gate, when you are getting out there to seek your fortune and...

9 is the final push for victory, the last mile, and everything finally coming together.

10 is the successful outcome, the realisation of everything that has gone before, the end of one cycle and the start of another.

Numerology Table

MEANING	PHRASE	VISUAL
1. Beginnings	1 Stand Alone	Me, Myself and 1
2. Cooperation	2's Company	2 swans = heart silhouette
3. Expansion	3's A Crowd	3 = breasts to feed a baby
4. Security	4 Walls	A house has 4 walls
5. Activity	5 Alive	5 is a hive of activity
6. Communication	6 Is Social	6 = eye, ear or telephone
7. Spirituality	7th Heaven	7 is a question mark
8. Inspiration	8 The Gate	8 is a lightbulb
9. Changes	Plan 9	9 is a higher level 6
10. Success	10 Out Of 10	You aced it!

Numerology Chart

NUMBER	CALCULATION	MEANING
Destiny	Top row	Current forces
Root	Bottom row	Overall trend
Opportunity	^ Highest - Lowest	Future signs
Resonant	Repeating digits	Trends over time
Absent	Missing digits	Missing forces

Number Chart Recap

See if you can answer these questions before you move on

Get Your Facts Straight

1. Which part of a Client's mobile phone number do you NOT use to create their chart?

2. How do you calculate a Client's Destiny and Lucky Root numbers?

3. What is the difference between these two numbers?

4. How do you calculate a Client's Number Of Opportunity?

5. How do you handle single digits in a row, when the other row still has digits to add?

6. What can you do with Resonant Numbers to make them more visible to the Client?

7. How can you tell which time period a Resonant Number belongs to?

8. How would you explain the concept behind Absent Numbers to a Client?

Get Your Mouth In Gear

Come up with something to say to each of these four Clients based on the three main numbers of their Numerology Chart. Speak out loud, and in your own words.

	Name	Destiny	Lucky Root	Opportunity
9.	Victor	5	2	7
10.	Glynis	1	8	4
11.	Hugo	6	9	3
12.	Kate	8	5	2

Yours And Mine

Your Chart - Get Your Mouth In Gear

Create a chart for yourself, based on your own mobile number and lucky number. Underline the resonant numbers, take note of any absent numbers, and then give yourself a reading. Treat yourself as a Client and explain everything, speaking out loud as you go.

- Do the meanings behind your Destiny and Lucky Root numbers hold any special relevance to you?

- Does the meaning behind your Number Of Opportunity align with your future goals?

- Do your Resonant Numbers match your experiences up to this moment in your life?

- Do your Absent Numbers hold any clues to how you might best proceed?

My Chart - Get Your Mouth In Gear

For obvious reasons I'm unwilling to share my mobile number publicly. What I can offer, however, are the last six digits of my number with the prefix removed (221974) and my lucky number 36. Create a chart for me and compare your chart with mine. Explain my chart to me as if I were there, referring to your own chart often. Speak out loud, and for as long as possible.

- Do our Destiny and Lucky Root numbers align in any way and, if not, how do they differ?

- Based on our Number Of Opportunity, how could we help each other reach our goals?

- Do our Resonant Numbers share any similarities or differences?

- If we were a team, how could we help each other encourage the forces missing in our lives?

N8 Mobile Number Reading Example

Here's an example reading I could give, using the numbers from the ongoing example starting on page 229. Because of the minor calculations involved, Numerology readings take longer to set up than Graphology readings. This gives me ample time to collect my thoughts as I create the Client's chart. As before, you will need to imagine this as a two-way conversation.

'So, we've totalled the digits in your mobile and lucky number, and arrived at what looks like a fraction, with a top number of 10, and a bottom number of 9. The number 10 at the top is your destiny number, and shows the influences during your current life cycle, things that have happened over the last few years, that kind of thing. The number below it is 9, your lucky root. This is a number that's been influencing you for longer, and is obviously a lot more personal.

'Your Destiny Number of 10 is a good number actually, and marks the end of a cycle. It's also a pretty successful number, and has a lot to do with completion. It indicates that, in the greater scheme of things at least, there's been some good stuff going on in your life. Does that make sense?

'Underlying all that is your Lucky Root 9, which has cast its influence a lot longer. The number 9 is all about change so my question to you is, do you feel like there's been a lot of change in your life over the last few years?

'Ok, so when you take the larger of these numbers away from the other, you get your Number Of Opportunity, and 9 from 10 equals 1, which we'll write down here. The Number Of Opportunity is a number you need to look out for in the future, and is all about new beginnings and fresh starts. Have you been thinking of doing anything new or going down a different path lately?

'Numbers that repeat are called Resonant Numbers, and influence everything around them. Of all the numbers we can see, its obvious the number 9 repeats, so I will underline these digits. The number 9, and the idea of change, is working in the background in some way. Numbers to the right of the chart are fairly current, so this trend could be ongoing. Do you feel that you could be in a moment of change?

'There are two number 3s near the front of the chart, and the number 3 represents expansion. There may well have been great excitement, and many ideas, at the start of your current cycle. The number 3 also represents birth, whether it's a child or a business venture. 3 can also mean growth, so it could allude to a deeper kind of development.

'There are two 2s and two 6s in your chart, indicating cooperation and communication, respectively. These often go hand in hand, and could indicate joint ventures and particularly fruitful partnerships. The 2s appear a little earlier than the 6s, so cooperation at the start of your current cycle could have evolved into a more communicative phase as things moved on. Have you been in some kind of business partnership? And has communication played a strong role in your recent past?

'Well, it could be your relationships, but as you've said, you've had a lot of pressure at work over the last few years.

'What's very interesting is, although almost every number is represented in your chart, the number 7 is nowhere to be seen. Absent Numbers can help us reflect on anything we may be missing in our lives. The number 7 is all about spirituality, so I wondered if you're a spiritual person or not.

'Well, I guess it's not just about spirituality, but about needing more time to work on yourself. Now your current cycle is ending, the number 7 could indicate a need to collect your thoughts, and energy, for your next adventure.'

A few notes on this example:

- I start the reading as soon as both the Destiny Number and Lucky Root have been calculated. This gets things off to a flying start and helps gives the reading some shape when I reveal the Client's Number Of Opportunity later.

- I report what I see in the numbers, and give the Client time to think. Numerology uses broader strokes than most other oracles, so there's more to process for the Client. I let ideas and concepts sink in before moving on.

- Only the Client's reaction to their Numerology trends can give me an insight into their character. I am not telling them what they are like. I am suggesting what may have been happening in their lives.

- Numerology readings are less contradictory than oracles such as Palmistry or Graphology, making it a lot easier for the Client to keep quiet during a Numerology reading. I need to push them for a reaction more often.

- I tell Clients to look out for Absent Numbers in their future, but avoid making predictions of any kind.

NUMEROLOGY RECAP & QUIZ

Here is a randomised collection of Numerology questions from each recap. As Numerology only has ten numbers to work with, there are not as many questions in this chapter as the others. As before, try to answer ALL these questions out loud and in your own words.

Remember these simple rules:

- Recent trends are found in The Destiny Number, derived from the most recent number in a Client's life

- Lifetime trends are found in the Lucky Root, derived from the Client's lucky number

- Taking one from the other, you are left with the Number Of Opportunity, things to look out for

- Resonant Numbers are digits that occur more than once in a chart, with a timeline from left to right

- Absent Numbers are digits that are missing from the chart, and can signify gaps in a Client's life

THE BIG NUMEROLOGY QUIZ

Get Your Facts Straight

Test your recall before moving on to the GYMIG section of this recap.

1. How will you remember what the number 4 signifies?

2. This is the number 7. It looks curious, but what does it rhyme with?

3. What does 8 rhyme with?

4. Why do you think the number 2 signifies love?

5. 9 is very nearly a 10. How can that help us remember its meaning?

6. The number 6 looks like several things to help you remember its meaning. What are they?

7. The number 5 rhymes with something that buzzes. What is it?

8. How can the number 2 help us remember the significance of the number 3?

9. 10 signifies success, but what else can it mean?

10. Which number makes you think of a lightbulb moment?

11. The 6 changes to a 9 once inverted. How is that significant?

12. What object has 4 Walls?

13. Which two numbers represent success and new beginnings?

14. Only one digit resembles a question mark. Which is it?

15. The numbers 2 and 3 can be remembered using a pair of well-known phrases. What are they?

16. What number do you think of when you imagine a bee returning home?

17. 6 is Social, but what three things does the number 6 look like?

18. The number 1 is closely tied to the number 10. But why?

19. What two animals can be used to remember the meaning of the number 2?

20. In what way are the number 1 and the number two similar?

Get Your Mouth In Gear

Come up with something to say to each of these four Clients based on the three main numbers of their Numerology Chart. Speak out loud, and in your own words.

	Name	Destiny	Lucky Root	Opportunity
9.	Walter	8	3	2
10.	Agatha	4	1	9
11.	Miguel	5	7	6
12.	Fiona	1	9	4

N9 Numerology Reading Practice

Get Your Mouth In Gear #1

Create a chart for each of these mobile numbers. Speak out loud as you go, as if explaining each chart to a Client. Don't worry too much about giving a reading just yet. Focus on the creation of each chart itself.

1. 02458 229756

2. 01718 936109

3. 09956 114487

4. 05653 353485

Get Your Mouth In Gear #2

Give each of these Clients a reading out loud based on the numbers above, considering each Client's gender, age and background.

Edward, Male, 32–Recently divorced, bald, young dress sense, open and chatty

Holly, Female, 23–Just finished university, short cropped hair, conservatively dressed, reserved

Alan, Male, 45–Considering a career change, long hair, ageing hippy, loud and overly talkative

Molly, Female, 39–Entrepreneur, red head, power dressing, quick-witted and astute

> **TOP TIP:** See the Bringing The Lines Together page 139 in the Palmistry Chapter, for some useful ideas on comparing lines. These same ideas can be used when comparing numbers.

N11 Numerology Conclusion

Numerology is more abstract to Clients than both Palmistry and Graphology, but the technique of using a story, similar to that employed by the James Bond Cold Reading, can help it connect on a deeper level.

As JBCR and Numerology are each based on a sequence of events, the two systems can be combined. For instance, the number one signifies Beginnings in Numerology, and the first line of JBCR reminds us of the extrovert / introvert concept so, should you run out of things to say using one system, you can draw from the other.

Another bonus is that Numerology is an easy gateway into Cartomancy. By treating the meanings of the four suits as Lenses across the numbers one to ten, you will have a working knowledge of over seventy-five percent of the deck. You can learn more about Lenses in the Hot Or Not section of JBCR, and can read a brief treatise on Cartomancy in Bonus Section II near the end of this book.

You can also learn a different method of giving Numerology readings from my book **'Numerology - Numbers Past And Present With The Lo-Shu Square'**. It uses the same story approach as the one outlined here, so you will be up to speed in no time. The Lo-Shu square is a great system for giving fun and informative numerology readings, so I suggest you check it out. The book also includes a set of digital flash cards to aid in learning the meanings of the ten digits. You can download these from my website for free, with no purchase necessary. Print them onto index cards, or swipe through them on your phone or tablet. Your choice!

All the best, and may there be strength in your numbers!

BONUS SECTION

B1

STAR SIGNS

Most people know their star sign and have a grasp of its basic meaning, and it's not unusual for the topic of astrology to come up when giving a reading. Some Clients may even expect you to perceive their star sign intuitively. Clients that know more than most about these things may wonder why you never mentioned their star sign during a reading. Therefore, a basic grasp of the zodiac's signs, dates and meanings is not only useful, but essential.

The mere mention of star signs can be enough to get people talking. Friends love to compare the differences between their signs, and you will find few people that disagree with what their sign has to say about them. This is fortunate, as knowing a Client's star sign can put you at a distinct advantage as a reader. Knowing a Client's star sign, either in advance or during a reading, is akin to being handed a selection of truisms on a plate, with the bonus that the Client has most likely heard of, and agreed with, many of them before. There is also no better excuse to give a reading than to compare a Client's star sign to a Palmistry, Graphology, or Numerology reading. You may think you act like a Libra, but let us see if your palm agrees...

Although an explanation of the zodiac is well beyond the remit of this book, I will share here a method, using visualisation techniques similar to those found in James Bond Cold Reading, to recall the dates of each sign of the zodiac approximately 87% of the time. This is useful should you glean a potential Client's birthday, or overhear the month they were born in.

First, I'll teach you a way to associate an image with each month of the year. Then, through a simple process of visualisation, to combine each month image with its star sign image. The idea is that, the moment you recall the image of a month, its star sign follows. An 87% success rate is pretty good odds, especially for those with little or no experience of astrology.

Should you enjoy the method outlined here, you can find a more in-depth explanation in my book **'Star Signs–A Cool System For Remembering The Dates And Meanings Of The Twelve Signs Of The Zodiac'**.

THE MONTH IMAGES

There are twelve months of the year and twelve signs of the zodiac. As the names of the months are fairly abstract, we can make them more memorable using similar sounding words to create a mental image for each, such as Mayonnaise for the month of May.

Here are the twelve months of the year with their associated visualisations:

- January - Jam
- February - Brew
- March - Marsh
- April - Pill
- May - Mayonnaise
- June - Tune
- July - Lie
- August - Gust
- September - Sceptre
- October - Octopus
- November - No
- December - Dismember

Now let us run through each visualisation:

JAM sounds like the start of **JANuary**, so you have the idea of jam, in a pot or spread over something

BREW sounds like the second part of **feBRUary** so there is the idea of beer, perhaps in a glass or jug

MARSH sounds like **MARCH** which is fairly straightforward, some kind of boggy landscape

PILL sounds like the end of **aPRIL**, and could refer to some kind of headache tablet

MAYONNAISE of course starts with **MAY** so this is easy to remember, a simple jar of mayonnaise for example

TUNE sounds almost identical to **JUNE**, so you have the idea of whistling harmonies

LIE is based on the end sound of the month **juLY**, the idea of a pair of crossed fingers to represent lying

GUST is the end sound of **auGUST**, the idea of a gust of wind

SCEPTRE is based on the start sound of **SEPTember**, a sceptre being a long ornate staff held by kings

NO is quite simply the start of the word **NOvember**, and is the idea of a warning, such as a 'keep out' or 'no entry' sign

DISMEMBER sounds almost exactly like **DECEMBER**, a rather gruesome lack of legs or arms

Reading this list a few times can be enough to remember most of it, but let's do a few exercises to help fix it in our minds. Read the following list of months and associated images SLOWLY. Each time you read a month and its associated image, create a visualisation of the word as vividly as you can before moving on to the next one. Take your time, and just give each month and associated image enough time to sink in. If you have spent any time learning the lines from James Bond Cold Reading, you'll be well acquainted with this kind of thing. Keep reading and repeating, and you may well surprise yourself with how quickly you can digest it all.

Month Images Recap

IMAGINE #1

Repeat each one in your mind a few times before moving on to the next. Stare into space or close your eyes if you have to.

- January - Jam - JAMuary - a pot of jam
- February - Brew - feBREWary - a beer in a glass
- March - Marsh - MARSCH - a marshy bog
- April - Pill - aPrIL - a headache tablet
- May - Mayonnaise - MAYonnaise - a jar of mayonnaise
- June - Tune - TJUNE - whistling, harmonies
- July - Lie - juLIE - a fib, crossed fingers
- August - Gust - auGUST - a big gust of wind
- September - Sceptre - SCEPTember - an ornate staff
- October - Octopus - OCTOpus - an eight legged sea creature
- November - No - NOvember - a warning, no entry sign
- December - Dismember - DISCMEMBER - chopped off legs

Once you have read through this list in your mind, read the list again out loud before you move on. Try visualising each month for at least five seconds each.

IMAGINE #2

Now let's try the next exercise without looking at the previous list to see if you can recite it from memory. Do these in your head first.

- January goes with ...
- February goes with ...
- March goes with ...
- April goes with ...
- May goes with ...
- June goes with ...
- July goes with ...
- August goes with ...
- September goes with ...

- October goes with ...
- November goes with ...
- December goes with ...

Once you've done these in your head, try this exercise again out loud, taking a note of the months that slow you down or you find hard to remember. You may find your recall good after only one or two passes, but you have to be honest with yourself about those months that trip you up. If some months will not stick, take the time to go over them again.

Exercise 1

Once you can recall the months and their associated images, try completing these sentences.

- Gust is for ...
- Tune is for ...
- Lie is for ...
- Sceptre is for ...
- Dismember is for ...
- Brew is for ...
- Pill is for ...
- Mayonnaise is for ...
- Octopus is for ...
- No is for ...
- Marsh is for ...
- Jam is for ...

Read through the above list out loud again before you move on, filling in the month for each image as before.

The idea here is we're doing things in reverse, by thinking of a mental image first and then calling out its associated month. The similarities in the sounds of months and images should be enough for you to recall the months fairly easily. For instance, as soon as I think of the word Marsh I know it is associated with the month March, and as soon as I think of the word Jam I immediately think of January.

If you find you're still having problems, then you need a little more practice. Try writing the months and images down on paper, or recite them while you go about your everyday business. Make your visualisations as strong as possible, and don't be afraid to spend a good few seconds imprinting the months, and images, in your mind.

Exercise 2

Read through this list a few times, taking note of any months you find harder than others.

- **January** - Jam
- **February** - Brew
- **March** - Marsh
- **April** - Pill
- **May** - Mayonnaise
- **June** - Tune
- **July** - Lie
- **August** - Gust
- **September** - Sceptre
- **October** - Octopus
- **November** - No
- **December** - Dismember

Read through the above list out loud again before you move on, and then see if you can run through each month and its associated visual without looking.

MONTHS AND SIGNS

The month images should be embedded by now. We're now going to combine the month images with the star signs through a series of combined visualisations. Here are the months and their images alongside each star sign. Have a casual read through this list, and just think for a moment how you could connect each month's image with their corresponding star sign.

- **January** - Jam - Capricorn - The Ram
- **February** - Brew - Aquarius - The Water Bearer
- **March** - Marsh - Pisces - The Fish
- **April** - Pill - Aries - The Ram
- **May** - Mayonnaise - Taurus - The Bull
- **June** - Tune - Gemini - The Twins
- **July** - Lie - Cancer - The Crab
- **August** - Gust - Leo - The Lion
- **September** - Sceptre - Virgo - The Virgin
- **October** - Octopus - Libra - The Scales
- **November** - No - Scorpio - The Scorpion
- **December** - Dismember - Sagittarius - The Centaur

This can look abstract with the months, month images and star signs together, but with a little thought, we can combine each idea into one visualisation. We want to get to a place where, by recalling a month, we also recall its star sign image, and vice versa. For instance, we see a ram (Capricorn) with a jammy beard, and recall January or, by recalling the mayonnaise of May, we see a bull (Taurus) eating mayonnaise.

Imagine these next examples as vividly as you can, creating a strong mental image for each one. You will find this slightly harder to wrap your head around than the simple month visualisations, but you will still be surprised how quickly you can get it down.

Imagine each of these scenes as vividly as possible. Make them as vibrant, colourful, and active as you can. Don't just see them as static pictures. Bring them to life and imagine you were there.

IMAGINE #3

- **CAPRICORN**: Imagine a ram with a white beard covered in JAM standing in a grassy field
- **AQUARIUS**: Imagine a beautiful princess pouring BEER through the air into a lake from a large vase
- **PISCES**: Imagine two playful fish swimming in a MARSH
- **ARIES**: Imagine an angry white ram with fiery eyes taking a PILL for his migraine
- **TAURUS**: Imagine a strong-headed bull in a fenced field licking MAYONNAISE out of a jar
- **GEMINI**: Imagine two identical young twins holding hands in the air whistling a TUNE together
- **CANCER**: Imagine a big red crab on a sandy beach telling a LIE (crossing its claws as if fibbing)
- **LEO**: Imagine a great lion with a fiery mane blown by a GUST of wind as it surveys its territory
- **VIRGO**: Imagine an innocent young girl in a flowery field holding a SCEPTRE
- **LIBRA**: Imagine an empty pair of scales weighing nothing but air held by an OCTOPUS
- **SCORPIO**: Imagine a scorpion scuttling about on the sand near an oasis with a NO entry sign
- **SAGITTARIUS**: Imagine a centaur with no legs (DISMEMBER) firing a flaming arrow from a bow

Once you've got to the end of this list, go back and visualise each of them again. Try imagining them first as a painting, then a photograph, and then as a scene that you can walk into and around. Get your internal camera moving, and approach each visualisation from as many angles as you can.

TIME TO FORGET

If you have worked through every star sign exercise so far, it is definitely time for a mental break. I suggest forgetting (or attempting to forget) everything you've visualised in this section. Visual memories have a habit of sticking around, and it's hard to forget things once you have imagined them hard enough.

Months And Signs Recap

Exercise 3

Answer each of the following questions, focusing firstly on each question's month before recalling its star sign image.

- Which star sign has a beard covered in jam?
- Which star sign is pouring beer into a lake?
- Which star sign is swimming in a marsh?
- Which star sign is taking a headache pill?
- Which star sign is licking a jar of mayonnaise?
- Which star sign is whistling a tune in harmony?
- Which star sign is telling a lie?
- Which star sign is having its hair blown by a gust of wind?
- Which star sign is holding a sceptre?
- Which star sign is an octopus holding?
- Which star sign is holding a no entry sign?
- Which star sign has its legs missing?

You may find you can recall the visual image for a star sign, but cannot recall the name of the star sign itself, especially if you are new to the signs of the zodiac. If this is the case, focus on those signs whose names you find more difficult than others, and re-visualise them before trying the questions again.

You will notice that some signs are extremely well matched to the words given for each month:

- Not only is January easy to remember as JAM, it also rhymes with the Ram of Capricorn
- February has the word BREW, so it's easy to remember that it's Aquarius The Water Bearer pouring beer instead of water
- March has the word MARSH, so it's obvious that Pisces The Fish should swim in it
- November is simply the word NO. One sign you should not go near is Scorpio The Scorpion!

Exercise 4

Here are the same questions from the previous section in a different order. Don't stress about answering these questions, relax and see if the answers come to you.

- Which star sign has its legs missing?
- Which star sign is pouring beer into a lake?
- Which star sign is holding a sceptre?
- Which star sign is an octopus holding?
- Which star sign is swimming in a marsh?
- Which star sign has a white beard covered in jam?
- Which star sign is taking a headache pill?
- Which star sign is licking a jar of mayonnaise?
- Which star sign is having its hair blown by a gust of wind?
- Which star sign is holding a no entry sign?
- Which star sign is whistling a harmonious tune?
- Which star sign is telling a lie?

You should have the hang of this by now and hopefully, when you visualise any month word, its associated star sign should come to mind almost immediately. You can now learn about the 23rd day premise, a simple ploy to make up for the fact that star signs start and end around the fourth week of each month.

The 23rd Day Premise

Each star sign starts around the 23rd day of the month, and ends around the 22nd of the next month. This is a generalisation, as the start and end dates shift between the 19th and 23rd, depending on the month involved. The dates between the changeover from one star sign to another are called the cusp.

Actual Star Sign Dates

These are the actual dates for each star sign:

Capricorn	December 22 - January 19
Aquarius	January 20 - February 18
Pisces	February 19 - March 20
Aries	March 21 - April 19
Taurus	April 20 - May 20
Gemini	May 21 - June 20
Cancer	June 21 - July 22
Leo	July 23 - August 22
Virgo	August 23 - September 22
Libra	September 23 - October 22
Scorpio	October 23 - November 21
Sagittarius	November 22 - December 21

For our purposes, and to achieve almost 90% accuracy with as little memory work as possible, we are going to pretend that all signs start on the 23rd and run through to the 22nd of the next month.

Inaccurate Star Sign Dates

Using the 23rd Day Premise, our inaccurate list of star signs fall on these dates:

Capricorn	December 23 - January 22
Aquarius	January 23 - February 22
Pisces	February 23 - March 22
Aries	March 23 - April 22

Taurus	April 23 - May 22
Gemini	May 23 - June 22
Cancer	June 23 - July 22
Leo	July 23 - August 22
Virgo	August 23 - September 22
Libra	September 23 - October 22
Scorpio	October 23 - November 22
Sagittarius	November 23 - December 22

As you can see, Capricorn belongs mostly to January, but starts at the end of December, whereas Aquarius belongs mostly to February, but starts at the end of January. All star sign dates end in the months they inhabit the most, or their monthly majority.

Month Majority

Star sign dates can appear daunting, so let us focus on each sign's monthly majority:

Capricorn	January
Aquarius	February
Pisces	March
Aries	April
Taurus	May
Gemini	June
Cancer	July
Leo	August
Virgo	September
Libra	October
Scorpio	November
Sagittarius	December

As you can see, the 23rd Day Premise simplifies things greatly. Now let's put it to use.

Close But No Cigar

So how can we use the 23rd Day Premise? If all star signs started on the 23rd of their respective months, we'd know this much:

> **1.** If a birthday falls before the 23rd of any given month, its star sign is from the same month
> **2.** If a birthday falls on or after the 23rd of any given month, its star sign is from the next month

For Example:

- For a Client born on October 2nd, you would know their star sign was from the same month.
- For a Client born on December 28th, you would know their star sign is from the next month, January
- For a Client born on April 18th, you would know their star sign was from the same month
- For a Client born on July 24th, you would know their star sign is from the next month, August
- For a Client born on January 5th, you would know their star sign was from the same month

The basic rule is, use the current month's star sign before the 23rd, otherwise use the next month's sign.

With an understanding of the 23rd Day Premise and a head full of star sign visualisations, we can calculate any Client's star sign from their birth date 87% of the time and, on those occasions when you are wrong, you will only be one star sign out.

How to put The 23rd Day Premise into practice:

> 1. Somehow, learn of a Client's date of birth.
> 2. If the day they were born on is before the 23rd of the month, they take the star sign from the same month, otherwise for the month after.
> 3. Think of the word for the relevant month to recall its combined star sign image.

4. Either tell the Client their star sign, or use the traits from their star sign to enhance, or deliver, a reading.

Example One

A Straight Up Calculation

A Client tells you they were born on the 10th of July. They were born on the 10th which is before the 23rd, so you keep the month. The month image for July is LIE and you immediately see Cancer The Crab lying with its claws crossed. The Client is a Cancer, and you tell them their star sign without hesitation.

Example Two

A Reading Enhancer

Unbeknownst to them, you learn a Client was born on the 25th of January. The 25th is after the 23rd, so you use the next month, February. You think of the month image for February which is BREW. The moment you think of brew, you see Aquarius, The Water Bearer, pouring beer into a lake. The Client is an Aquarius.

During a palm reading for the same Client, you inject the reading with traits taken from their star sign and, with this added knowledge, the reading is perceived as being particularly insightful. Near the end of the reading, and to the Client's surprise, you ask whether they could be an Aquarius. You could, however, make no mention of their star sign at all, and use the their star sign's traits to enhance their reading.

Example Three

Hedging Your Bets

- You learn a Client was born on the 22nd of May but, as this date lies on the cusp, you know there is a chance your calculation could be wrong. They were born on the 22nd which is before the 23rd, so you keep the month. The month image for May is MAYONNAISE which conjures up a bull eating mayonnaise (Taurus), but you know that the Client's sign may well come from the next month, June, which brings with it the idea of twins whistling a TUNE together (Gemini). You tell the Client you are getting mixed messages and, during a reading, ask them whether they feel more like a Taurus or a Gemini.

This process can be quite rapid with a small amount of practice. The moment you have the correct month image, you can jump straight to the associated visualisation and see the relevant star sign. The only thing you need to remember is to go forwards a month if the day the person was born falls on, or after, the 23rd. As about three quarters of all star signs start before the 23rd, you will only be going forward to the next month a quarter of the time. As you can see from example three, you need to keep the cusp in mind, and to always hedge your bets should a Client's birthday fall between the 19th and 23rd of the month.

> **TOP TIP: Want to be more accurate? The acronym JASO (July, August, September, October) can help you remember that the star sign dates for the months July to November all start on the 23rd.**

Star Signs Recap

Answer these questions as if every star sign started on the 23rd of the month.

Exercise One

What are the star signs of the people born on the following dates?

1. 24th of January
2. 5th of February
3. 30th of March
4. 15th of April
5. 2nd of May

6. 9th of June
7. 24th of July
8. 1st of August
9. 25th of September
10. 20th of October
11. 30th of November
12. 4th of December

After attempting these twelve questions, you should be getting a feel for how the star signs overlap the end of one month and most of the next. You should also know whether or not you need to go forward a month.

Let us do things in reverse just once to make sure we are joining everything up properly in our minds. To do the next exercise, you are going to have to think of the mental image you have of a star sign, see the month word in that image, and then convert it back into its actual month.

Exercise Two

What month do the following star signs inhabit the most?

1. Capricorn
2. Sagittarius
3. Scorpio
4. Aries
5. Pisces
6. Aquarius
7. Cancer
8. Gemini
9. Taurus
10. Libra
11. Virgo
12. Leo

STAR SIGNS CONCLUSION

Star signs and horoscopes are as close as most people get to character readings and fortune-telling. You will be expected to know at least as much about the various signs of the zodiac as your Clients. If you have never studied star signs, I hope this section helps you commit their dates to memory. If you already know their meanings but struggle with their dates, I hope this method helps you.

Although this method can be learnt fairly quickly, memories have a tendency to fade. Only spaced repetition can prevent them vanishing altogether. If you're using this method day in, day out, it shouldn't be a problem, but you'll most likely need to revisit this method, and its visualisations, from time to time. However, if you repeatedly come back to it, you'll likely never forget it.

The full star signs method can be found in my book **'Star Signs–A Cool System For Remembering The Dates And Meanings Of The Twelve Signs Of The Zodiac'**. A set of digital flash cards accompany the book, which can be downloaded for free from my website, with no purchase necessary. As the basic method is the same as outlined here, you may find these cards useful for revision. These can be printed on index cards, or you can swipe through them on your phone or tablet. It's up to you.

I wish you luck on your star signs journey!

www.coldreading.co

B2

Cartomancy

If you've come this far, there's a good chance you have a basic understanding of Numerology, and are familiar with the number meanings. This is fortuitous, as Cartomancy and Numerology are close cousins. The suits in a deck act as Lenses for the spot cards, so once you have learnt these four concepts you will be well on the way to understanding the meaning behind 40 out of a deck's 52 cards.

Should you enjoy the method outlined here, you can find a more in-depth explanation in my book **'Cartomancy–Fortune Telling With Playing Cards'**.

You can read more about lenses in James Bond Cold Reading page 81.

Suit Meanings

The red suit meanings are self explanatory. Diamonds revolve around money and finance, and Hearts concern love, relationships, and romance.

- **DIAMONDS** - Money
- **HEARTS** - Love

The black cards are more abstract than the red cards. Clubs are all about work and career, whereas Spades are about obstacles and difficulties.

- **CLUBS** - Work
- **SPADES** - Obstacles

> TOP TIP: Imagine tripping on a carelessly dropped SPADE in the road whilst walking to your job at a Working Men's CLUB.

Card Meanings And Examples

To understand each card's unique attribute, we view each number's meaning through the Lens of each suit. I won't list every card here as that would be missing the point–the idea is to come up with meanings for each card yourself. Riffing on these combined concepts, rather than having a preconceived notion of each card's meaning, keeps things fresh and helps avoids the slog of learning each card by rote.

 **You can learn all about riffs and riffing in Chapter Four, page 50 of James Bond Cold Reading.**

Look through these brief examples and take a moment to see how I have used number meanings and suits in tandem. You will need to expand on these ideas in your own words, so grab the spot cards from a deck, and riff on single cards until you have run out of things to say. As always, Get Your Mouth In Gear.

Examples

Three Of Diamonds

With the expansion and new creation of the three, and the power and success of diamonds, this card stands out as a card showing new ventures taking shape.

Nine Of Diamonds

With the dynamic nine signifying things moving rapidly and successfully in the right direction with a current project, and the financial success of diamonds, this card is extremely fortuitous and shows the rapid and rewarding developments of existing undertakings.

Ten Of Diamonds

Signifying the successful completion of a project or existing life cycle, with the rewards and power of diamonds, this is a tremendously auspicious card. Like all tens, it is about completion and, therefore, the end of one cycle and the start of another.

Five Of Clubs

With the organic growth of the five with the work aspect of clubs, this card brings to mind the idea of things taking shape at work - from solid foundations, things are starting to grow and develop.

Nine Of Clubs

With the nine signifying things coming to fruition, and the social and work aspects of clubs, this card is a strong indicator of work plans coming together and social engagements taking a front seat.

Ten Of Clubs

With the end of a cycle and the goals being reached, with the work ethic of clubs, it is no surprise that this is possibly one of the best work related cards in the deck, the completion of long-term projects and successful ventures.

Two Of Hearts

We know the two is about partnerships and sharing, and with the Hearts influence, also about love and pleasure, it is no surprise to find that the two of hearts is one of the most romantic cards in the pack and is a strong indicator of good relationships and happy marriages.

Three Of Hearts

With the idea of partnerships bearing fruit, and the love and romance aspect of hearts, this card cannot help but be a romantic card but with the added possibility of love turning into much more–a child on the horizon, perhaps? Or if not romance, the development of partnerships into fruitful relationships that go much deeper.

Seven Of Hearts

With the mystical and higher thinking seven, and the love aspect of hearts, this is a very spiritual card and can mean a breakthrough in all things spiritual, or of pure matters of the heart and soul–the happiness that can only come from within. Or above!

Nine Of Spades

With nine signifying great movement near the end of a project and the spades signifying obstacles, this card shows that the last few steps of a current endeavour may well be extremely challenging and one should look out for last-minute snags and surprises.

Ten Of Spades

With the ten being all about the successful completion of goals, yet spades signifying hurdles and fights, this card is possibly the most conflicted in the deck. As it stands, it is quite hard to read this card alone and care must be taken to see this card in context with the rest of the reading. One positive aspect of this card is that the ten is the end of a cycle and that after times of great upheaval comes the chance to start anew.

The Four Aces

The Aces are all about the energy of new starts and beginnings, and of raw drive and willpower. They energise the suits they are coupled with: The Ace of Diamonds is about the pure force of money and power, the Ace of Clubs is all about the strength and determination of work and growth, the Ace of Hearts is the essence of love and emotions, and the Ace of Spades is the power of the warrior to take on anything. These cards are naïve, representing the raw power of each suit before steps have been taken, and affect all the surrounding cards with their idealistic and unquestioned power.

Face Cards

The face cards in a deck refer to the people in our lives. The Jacks represent younger people of no particular sex, but may also indicate news. The Queens and Kings represent older women and men, or those in authority.

HEART face cards represent friends, lovers and family
DIAMOND face cards represent people with money or influence
CLUB face cards represent people in the work place
SPADES represent people who get in the way

As with the spot cards, the face cards reflect the concepts behind each suit. For instance, Spades represent obstacles, so a face card Spade is someone blocking the way.

Reading Examples

A simple way to structure a reading is to have a Client shuffle a deck and pick three cards at random. Laying these cards in a row from left to right you have their past, present and future cards. By looking at these cards, and examining the way they interact with each other, you can come up with a pretty interesting reading using just what you have learned from this short chapter. There now follows two example readings, using three cards each.

> **TOP TIP: With a three card reading, it is useful to use the idea that each card influences the previous card. So card two influences card one, and card three influences card two.**

Example One

Three Of Clubs / Six Of Diamonds / Four Of Spades

The reading starts with the Three of Clubs, which is all about ideas taking shape in and around work–the expansion idea of of the number Three with the influence of the Club, the work and socialising suit. With the Three of Clubs as the focus and the Six of Diamonds as the influence, we have the positive and strong ideas of communication and money. Maybe things are looking up regarding these work ideas taking shape, and if there has not been news about an injection of money as yet, it could come soon. As the Six is about communication and the Diamonds are about money and power, this is all quite a good influence on the Three of Clubs.

Moving on to the Six of Diamonds, we can see that this is influenced by the Four of Spades. The four is home life related, and as a Spade, this spells trouble at home, influencing the communication and money aspect of the Six of Diamonds. Perhaps there is some problem with work creating friction at home, or maybe the sources of the money are themselves being restricted by home life and other commitments. Whatever it is, it is obviously something that has to be sorted out before things can move on.

Example Two

Five Of Spades / Four Of Hearts / Jack Of Diamonds

The reading starts with the Five of Spades, the five signifying growth at home and in things that are already formed, but as it is a Spade, this is a problem with development, and could mean there is some kind of stagnation going on. With the focus on the Five of Spades and the influence of the Four of Hearts, we have the stability of the four with love and warmth of the Heart coming to bear on this problem. This is not a bad thing, and it looks like whatever is getting stuck somewhere is going to be helped with loved ones at home.

With the focus on the Four of Hearts and with the influence of the Jack of Diamonds, we know that there's a young person involved who is responsible for this stability and help. This could be an outside influence or could be a member of the family. If it is an outside influence, then their help could be monetary, and if it's family, then their powerful influence could be of the helping and healing kind.

The Jack could also be news, possibly involving a young person, that is part of this helping and stabilising Four of Hearts. Maybe news will come from someone that is expected but has yet to be known, and it is this that eases the symptoms of the Five of Spades.

Cartomancy Conclusion

I hope this overview of Cartomancy has given you some food for thought. If you've learnt the basic number meanings from the Numerology section, and are sufficiently versed in riffing from the hip, you'll find Cartomancy a breeze. Also, you can use the numbers to trigger concepts from James Bond Cold Reading too, should you wish. With all that under your belt, there is no excuse to run out of things to say once the cards are on the table.

If you're interested in learning more about Cartomancy, you could do worse than read my book **'Cartomancy–Fortune Telling With Playing Cards'**, an in-depth treatise on giving playing card readings. My Cartomancy book uses the same method found here, so if you have enjoyed learning about Cartomancy from these few pages, you will love the book. I hope you get the chance to check it out.

Enjoy, and may the cards be forever in your favour!

B3

Cold Reading As Effect

This essay first appeared in The James Bond Cold Reading 2007, and shows how JBCR can elevate a simple card trick into a powerful demonstration of mind-reading. I have removed some conjuring references to avoid upsetting the book's original audience, and rewritten descriptive sections for clarity. The conversational text remains largely unchanged from the original.

A great way to illustrate the power of cold reading is to use something as simple as the oldest trick in the book; pick-a-card. It does not have to be a card, of course. It could be a number, a colour, a word, or a host of other things one could think of. However, many of us know how to perform this childhood card trick, so it illustrates the technique perfectly. In this section, a fictitious character named Chris Reader will present himself as a non-psychic entertainer who purports to use scientific methods, such as body language and psychological profiling, to glean information on his subjects.

Certain conditions must be met for cold reading to be truly convincing, so let us first discuss when cold reading will not work. Imagine you have picked a card at random from a deck but, unbeknown to you, I have gleaned the suit and value of your card using my favourite conjuring method. I could reveal your card after a suitably long and suspenseful pause, but that is about it, as the random nature of your choice prevents me from framing the revelation as anything but a trick.

By changing the pick a card effect slightly, I can appear to give myself something to read. For example, I scatter the pack of 52 cards in front of you face up, turn my back, and tell you to think carefully about which card you will choose. When you have chosen, I turn to face you and, after a few moments where I appear to assess your clothes, posture and demeanour, I triumphantly announce the very card you are thinking of.

Because I gave you a free choice, I can suggest that a series of subconscious cues led me to your card. Of course, I knew the card you picked already because I cheated, but I can at least attempt to frame the effect as an example of my ability to read people.

Unfortunately, scratching my chin a few times before blurting out 'Ace Of Spades' does not constitute a cold reading. I have to prove beyond doubt my intuition goes far deeper than accusing you of liking heavy rock based on your choice of card. Remarks such as '...I can tell from your nose stud and long hair you chose the Ace Of Spades' sound more like post-justification than cold reading. During a cold reading, I must appear to tell you facts about yourself I could not possibly know.

Here is our humble pick-a-card trick scripted around the concepts of the twelve Classic Reading lines. Let us imagine that our imaginary spectator Pam is not particularly responsive or forthcoming to our host, Chris Reader. During this imaginary dialogue, Chris uses all twelve classic reading concepts in sequence. See if you can spot them.

Chris Reader: *'Hi my name's Chris Reader and I'd like to try a little experiment with you if I may. I've got a pack of cards here and as you can see, like all packs, we have the spades, hearts, diamonds and clubs, as well as the numbers one to ten and the face cards Jack, Queen and King. I'm going to hand you the pack, and if you could I would like you to keep cutting the pack over and over again like this, ok?'*

(performer hands cards to Pam)

'While you're doing that, I'd like you to think of all the numbers in your life that have a special significance for you, the colours that surround you every day, and the faces that make you happy. As you keep cutting the cards, let your mind drift and, in doing so, allow your thoughts to settle on a card that you think might have some significance for you. Don't rush this, it may take some time for a card to reveal itself to you, but please, keep it to yourself. I don't want to know what it is just yet.'

'When you have settled on a card, please stop cutting the cards and

place the pack back on the table face down. I will turn my back before you do this, so please let me know when you have finished, but take as long as you like. I need you to choose the card and the card to choose you, so please take your time.'

(The performer turns away from Pam. Pam finally thinks of a card and puts the cards face down onto the table.)

Pam: '*OK, I've done that.*'

Chris Reader: '*You've finished? Good. Now just so that everyone else here can know what card it is you're thinking of too, and so I don't overhear anything, can you just turn cards face up one at a time into another pile and stop when you get to your card? Thanks, and when you do come to the card you were thinking of, can you please show it to everyone here and then put it in your pocket so there has no way I could see it? Tell me when you've done that. Good, and can someone else collect up the cards so that no cards are to be seen anywhere? Thanks, let me know when all the cards are put away and I'll turn back round.*'

(Note: Chris now knows the card that Pam is thinking of. If you find this impressive, and want to learn more about this kind of thing, you will have to do some research. Shenanigans such as this is way beyond the scope of this book, but I wish you luck should you find yourself on a magical adventure.)

Pam: '*Done it!*'

(The performer turns to face Pam)

Chris Reader: '*So Pam, I don't know much about you, so to help me do this I am going to need you to be fairly open and honest with me, ok? If we could just talk about you a little bit, that would be great. Now I've noticed that you didn't take much prompting to take part in this experiment, so I think I would be right in saying that you're quite an outgoing type of person. What I'm noticing already, however, is that being put on the spot like this isn't entirely natural for you, is it? I think you're the kind of person who enjoys these kinds of get-*

togethers, but you also like your home comforts and could just as happily sit at home with your feet up. Even though secretly you can be a little shy, you do like being the centre of attention as you are now, don't you?'

Pam: (laughs) '*Yes.*'

Chris Reader: '*Have you always been like that?*'

Pam: '*Kind of.*'

Chris Reader: '*I get the feeling that this could have been like some kind of defence mechanism perhaps, and as you grew up, you felt a need to assert yourself, but the shyness never left you totally. I get a sense that you still get a little nervous around certain people, but you've learned to bottle it up and in fact 'being loud' has helped you in life. You're certainly a colourful character, and I'd hazard a guess that you thought of a red card. Is that correct?*'

Pam: '*Yes.*'

Chris Reader: *Ok we're getting somewhere now, I'm starting to build a picture up in my mind. I'd say from looking at your immaculate appearance, you can tend to be overly critical of yourself. It must take a lot of effort to look that good! There have probably been issues in the past with people being jealous of you, but that's unfair, as they don't know what you've been through. Being critical of yourself, however, can sometimes mean you're rather critical of others, even though most of the time you don't let on, other people can be rather disappointing sometimes! Would that be a fair assumption?*

Pam: '*Yeah, well...*'

Chris Reader: '*But you have been let down in the past, haven't you?*'

Pam: 'Yeah...'

Chris Reader: '*You see, you can be quite headstrong and this is one of your strengths. You like to know what's what on your own terms, and* you don't just believe what everyone is telling you - you like to find things out for yourself. But because of these let downs you've learned to keep things to yourself a lot more, wouldn't you say?'

Pam: *'Uh-uh, I guess I know when to shut up!'* (laughs)

Chris Reader: *'Yes, and this is why this is proving quite difficult? You're really not giving too much away. In fact, it's not so much about what you're saying, it's about what you're not saying! But I think because of this you didn't pick a people card like a Jack, Queen or King did you, you chose a number card I think, is that correct? Yes, I thought to, you see, you are a people person to most people, but there is an awful lot going on under the bonnet than most people would give you credit for.'*

'Now I would imagine that this has presented all kind of challenges for you, but you do seem to have a heart of gold, I can really feel that and I know I'm not alone in that sense, I'm sure that everyone here can feel that. I mean, along with the being critical of yourself, you know you do have faults, but you are able to compensate for them in other ways, wouldn't you say?'

Pam: *'Yeah sure, we all have our problems...'*

Chris Reader: *'But wouldn't you say that in many ways this drives you forward? I see you as a problem solver. You are able to see quite clearly what you are like and move on, almost using your shortcomings as fuel to do good things for yourself and others. We all have our faults, but I think you have a unique way of dealing with yours in the way you can turn them to your advantage. It's this kind of thinking that also made me think you chose a number card. But also the fact that you have this soft, almost nurturing side makes me think you probably settled on a heart, is that correct?'*

Pam: *'Yes!'*

Chris Reader: *'Ok, so for some reason your personality talked to you and whispered a heart-shaped number card to you. Now this could be a low number, a middle number, or a high number. No, don't smile too much, I don't want too many clues!'*

Pam: (laughs)

Chris Reader: *'I would say that with all we have talked about, sometimes you can wonder if you've made some of the right decisions in your life...'*

Pam: *'Er, not really...'*

Chris Reader: *'But you have wondered what might have happened if you'd have done things differently?'*

Pam: *'Well, yes, sometimes...'*

Chris Reader: *'This leads me to believe that the word achievement means something to you, in as much as you have your own goals you want to achieve. These may not always seem much to other people, but they mean a lot to you. In fact, other people can tend to see you as erratic, but in fact you like change, so you do things the way you see fit.'*

Pam: *'Yes I like to do things in my own sweet way.'*

Chris Reader: *'Talking about this achievement thing, I would say that occasionally you can set your sights too high and can sometimes feel a little let down. Is that true?'*

Pam: *'Well, kinda...'* (smiling)

Chris Reader: *'Sometimes you can tend to live in your own world and find yourself coming back to earth with a bump. But saying that, you do have the stamina to hit back when you need to and although some of your aspirations are a bit far fetched, you do have an uncanny knack for pulling some of them off.'*

Pam: *'Yes, er...'*

Chris Reader: *'So I'm just having a guess here based on what we've* *talked about. I would say you went for a high card, like a nine or a ten. I think you probably thought of the ten of hearts.'*

Pam: '*Yes!*'

Chris Reader: '*Thank you for being such a wonderful accomplice!*'
In this dialogue, Chris Reader uses most of the techniques we have already discussed. The most important thing he does is place great emphasis on the selection process, expounding on the idea that Pam's card is a psychological choice. This guarantees that any cold reading line he may use can be connected to the card, and therefore, Pam. Emphasis is placed squarely on the method, and on the idea that Pam's chosen card is a reflection of her personality.

Unlike generalised character readings, Chris did not make too many future projections or give any kind of advice to Pam. Had Chris given a Palmistry reading, he would have had much more scope to delve into Pam's character. But with just one playing card chosen, and within the parameters of a performance, Chris was able to transform a simple pick–a–card trick into an insightful and engaging experience for everyone involved.

This essay copyright Julian Moore 2007

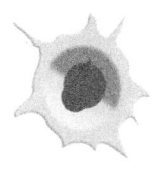

If you have enjoyed this book, please leave a rating and review on Amazon.

Thank You.

Julian

SPECIAL THANKS

Bill Cushman, for telling me to write more stuff

Enrique Enriquez, for the wonderful and unexpected Foreword

Richard Osterlind, for the killer quote

and

Nicky, for putting up with this nonsense

Printed in Great Britain
by Amazon